I would like to acknowledge the people that have helped me since coming forward.

I'm not sure whether or not people realize that even a few words of kindness and support have a huge effect on me when I'm sharing information like this.

When you decide to take a stand and share your truth, it comes with a hefty fee socially, especially when the truth goes against the mainstream.

To those who have been nothing but supportive of me this entire time, I want to say that every little act of reassurance is what has empowered me to come this far.

Alex, thank you for your feedback.

I would like to dedicate this book to my mom, Natalie Rodrigues, who taught me to be myself and to not bend to the fluid wills of society. To appreciate being an oddball. The last cookie on the baking sheet that is an unusual shape. To embrace being special. It turns out she was right all along.

It is fitting that this book was completed on Mother's Day 2023.

I would also like to say that without my great friend, Jackie Kenner, none of this would have been possible. She has been an amazing person to work with on every project and is absolutely brilliant.

And lastly, I would like to thank my family - Tara, and the girls. They are the reason that I stopped doubting myself. Because they needed me to be someone worthy.

Every man should be so lucky.

CONTENTS

PREFACE

The thing about this book is that it requires some buy in. My first book, *Ceres Colony Cavalier,* laid the groundwork for taking in what comes next. Anyone could pick up my first book and learn about the unknown Deep Space Program. As a reader, you could then decide for yourself what you believed. Each of us can and should always be assessing information and making up our own minds about what is true.

But if you can't find the truth in book one, I'm afraid I'm about to lose you even more. Which is a reality I've come to accept. These are my experiences. To publicize my twenty year tour in the face of scrutiny and ridicule was hard to do, and continues to be hard. But I felt like the public deserved to know and that to silence myself was to give power to the people and corporations that did this to me and that are doing this to others. But now, to share the part of my story that I've been holding back up until this point, this is for me. This is take it or leave it. This is what happened to me *inside* of that timeline.

And as a reader, you can and should still decide for yourself what you believe.

- Tony Rodrigues

FOREWORD BY TONY

When I first went public with the account of my abduction in 2016, the landscape of what was going on in the larger paranormal and UFO truther community was much different. There were others that spoke out before me that had amassed huge audiences. In my own mind, I was thinking to myself that I was only adding credibility to what had already been said. I thought that I would have an interview or two and then return to my seat in the audience. Then others would come forward and tell their accounts too. These would all support the accounts of the ones doing the disclosing full time, or professionally. I knew that the things I remembered experiencing were not going to be palatable for the majority of people. The average person really gets a bit of "TMI" from my account if we're being honest.

That being said, I had absolutely no intention of writing a book, having a website, or having my own show. Especially not of standing in front of a live audience and explaining that children are abducted and go through what I have gone through. I did intend to make my story known. I wanted them–the Greys, and the humans up there–to know that I did remember and that I do remember. The tired, sad, pathetic excuse they parroted to me time and time again as they disregarded my sovereignty was that, "I wasn't going to remember this anyway." But I did remember and that excuse did not justify their behavior in any way.

I beat them. I REMEMBER YOU, ASSHOLES. And I've told the world. Not even the shame could stop me. It's a victory for me in many ways.

However, people were really eager for a book.

"Tony you remember so much, please write it into a book."

When Youtube started taking down interviews of me and others like me, I thought to myself, "Oh God, all the work I've done sharing it and now it can just get deleted."

Suddenly, the wind shifted to my back. Andulairah had been working with me, transcribing recordings I sent very sporadically, for years. I would email her recordings when I had the grit to get them out of myself. Then I met Jackie who happened to have a Degree in Literature and a Masters in Communications. Plus she knew the whole story and how important it was–and things kinda fell together. We got *Ceres Colony Cavalier* out. It was a linear account of what happened to me, though it was made up mostly of the things interview hosts had asked me in live interviews.

I'm not sure if I realized until we got into the thick of the book that I was writing parts of my story based on things people had shown interest in. The cherry picked questions. But I finally included my own homage to the relationships I had during those years. No one had ever seemed to care to ask, "Who did you love when you were up there?" Or at least it was very rare. That part was important to me to share.

The book felt like and still feels like I am exposing a personal diary with the public. And I have certainly had my share of ridicule.

This next book is even worse on that front. It's made from personal, very secret things I don't even tell my best friends because it's so easy to shoot down, so easy to dismiss and ridicule. There's no proof. There is no other testimony to cross reference. No accurate description of places I remember and then going to confirm the locations, as I had done in Seattle in 2016. Nothing. It's a raw, blatant mess of vague, fuzzy, fragmented memories.

Some will probably read this book and do backflips, maybe some won't even finish it. I'm sure some will hate it, and they'll also surely take the time to let me know.

But.

Fuck it.

While I have five minutes of attention and a crowd asking for an encore, I can share this too. And not take it to the grave and somehow just release it all, letting death be the final way of getting it off my chest. Allowing only the Earth to receive my truth. Possibly one day in the future this becomes provable - who knows.

But for the reader, be advised. This is not *Ceres Colony Cavalier 2.*

I don't expect this account to be something that changes anything in the grand scheme of ET disclosure. Nor is it meant to be. For now, it's a demonstration of what consciousness technology is truly capable of.

A reminder that what goes on behind your dominant eye is more precious than gold and treated as such by countless worlds.

Not because it's Holy, but because it's talented.

Every drop of us is genius. Not me.

Us.

Every one of us. Everything. Conscious.

Genius.

FOREWORD
BY JACKIE

When I first heard Tony's story, I found it interesting (to say the *very* least), especially coming from a family of experiencers. The concept of a twenty year program filled a lot of gaps and answered a lot of questions I had around my own confused existence.

Tony and I bonded through the sharing of our experiences. Mostly his off-planet experiences and my medium experiences. That and our psychic training. Tony's training was forced through a trauma based mind control experiment and my training was both seemingly inherent and also self-taught. By inherent, I mean that I seemed to be psychic from birth. And then as I matured, I began to research how my abilities were possible. The result of doing so was that I inadvertently trained myself to be even more adept.

And Tony got it – he'd been trained too. It was amusing to shift between realms with a friend.

What he shared with me as we became close friends – and as we began to trust each other – is what led me to ultimately agree to ghostwrite and edit a trilogy of books with him. Our first book together, *Ceres Colony Cavalier,* was a labor of duty. In order to get to the content that I truly wanted to share with the world through this book, *Project Starmaker,* I knew that we had to first tell the original story that holds this smaller story within it.

And we had our work cut out for us. I had just married my husband, Neil, and I didn't know at the time, but I was pregnant with a baby boy and we had just purchased a duplex that required a double gut renovation. All of this was happening in the final weeks of editing and eventually publishing the book. By the time *Ceres Colony Cavalier* was released, I was exhausted on every level.

Mentally, the sole act of writing a book is draining. I believe this is why many people dream of the accomplishment, but only a fraction of those people make it to print. Emotionally, fleshing out the details of each story within the pages of *Ceres Colony Cavalier* over and over until I was sure we were making sense was disturbing. Spiritually, as I embarked on the journey of bringing a soul from the unseen world to the earth through my pregnancy, I was heartbroken to know in my heart that what Tony had endured was possible for any child on earth.

I retracted from everything when the book came out. I needed to heal, but I didn't even know it. In fact, I think at the time, what I felt most was anger. I wasn't sure why– but I was *different* after that book.

It's an odd situation to say to most people, "Yeah I ghostwrote a book, don't read it. Very dark. Do not recommend it."

But at some point, roughly a year later, I felt ready to write again. So here we are.

This following content aligns with the reality of my life on earth and beyond, as a medium. Not necessarily Tony's story, as that is his alone, but the implications of what he shares. I hope you'll embrace it with an open mind. Chances are, you've experienced parts of it yourself.

I've always felt that the best punchline is a question. In movies, literature, pieces of art that verberate the soul–they all leave us questioning.

If I jump to the punchline of *Project Starmaker*, my hope is that this book leaves you questioning your beliefs about the universe. Is the reality that you hang your hat on actually the way things are going down?

I think you're reading this book because you know it's not.

KEY

At the end of some chapters, you will find additional commentary. Footnotes, so to speak. They will follow the below format.

Tony allowed Jackie to ask specific questions after the stories he shared. They will be at the end of respective chapters.

His responses will follow.

Any further commentary on Jackie's behalf will follow Tony's responses in the form of separate chapters, with the chapters published in a different font.

CHAPTER 1

The Creator and the Crackheads

The most common question I get asked about my first book, *Ceres Colony Cavalier,* is what happened in the hallway on Ceres, the one where I was taken from one twenty-year program into another?

A twenty year program is what we call the experience of being abducted, having your consciousness split through an advanced technology, serving twenty years in an alternate timeline both on and off planet Earth, then having your memories wiped through another advanced technology–before being returned to the time and place of your abduction within a matter of minutes. Seconds even, perhaps. Like nothing happened. Twenty years will not have passed by your own accord. But they happened in some stretch of time-space because time is not linear. And consciousness is beyond vast. It's malleable actually. Both massive and miniscule simultaneously, to assign human words to a non-human concept. But we'll get to that.

So I'll start this book from the hallway in Ceres.

But in order to start from there, I actually need to first start from Peru.

I was a few years into my twenty year program and at the time, I was being used as a psychic tool for drug smugglers in Peru. They were the Narcos, and they were moving massive shipments of cocaine paste to Columbia in a C-46 Commando plane. The paste was called basuco, which means something along the lines of "trash" in spanish. It was essentially the unrefined product of the cocaine process. I had been through a trauma based mind control program in order to prime my mind, or perhaps my soul, for expanded consciousness connections with other realms of existence. My handlers in Peru would drug me, take me to a near death state, and basically have me remote view whether or not our flight path was safe.

Remote viewing is the practice of gathering impressions about distant subjects, using only the mind. The remote viewer gives information about locations, people, events, or objects that are not within physical view and usually separated by distance or time, or by both distance and time—meaning past or future events.

My role was essentially to be an early warning alarm if the police were onto us, if we were getting off course, or if we were going to encounter bad weather–things like that. The smugglers had lost their previous plane before acquiring me and I assume I came with a hefty fee, so it must have been enough cocaine paste to be well worth it.

We boarded the plane in Boca Colorado, Peru, which wasn't called that at the time. It was called Puerto Tahuantinsuyo. My handler, Manuel, would administer an IV shortly after takeoff, which always upset me because there was often turbulence and he was no phlebotomist. The pilot was sketchy too. The first flight we took was his first flight ever. He was a crop duster in Puerto Maldonato prior to becoming a basuco flier. He was fat and had greasy, long hair. And he hated me.

We flew north about an hour and a half, into the state of Acre. As soon as we entered into Acre, I'd get the IV, which administered a very precise dose of a specific drug that brought me to a near death state. After receiving this dose, I'd lose consciousness and wake up at an airport in Santa Marta, Colombia. It was roughly seven hours later. I have learned since the publication of *Ceres Colony Cavalier* that the plane we flew was confiscated by the Peruvian Military in the 90's and is now parked off an airfield in Pucallpa. I found it on Google Maps, though I'm sure it will be scrubbed too, just like the town of Puerto Tahuantinsuyo.

When the drug was added to the IV, I lost consciousness almost immediately. At first, I remembered nothing. Just waking up in Colombia, on the tarmac next to the ocean in Santa Marta. But after the fourth or fifth time, I started to become aware of my experiences under the administered medication. It began to feel like I fell asleep, same as before, except I started waking up while under the drugs.

When I started waking up, I found myself in what could be described as "a dark room" with other "people" that I couldn't see. It was pitch black. I would enter the room in one corner, and these people, or things, would push me away from the place where I came in. I wasn't a physical form. I was more of a mental form. It was terrifying for me. While we didn't have bodies, my sense was that I was a child and they were all adults. Some of the things were aggressive. They had voices and they were telling me to get out of the way. Everyone was in a hurry and desperate to get to the spot where I came into the room. It was the equivalent of a small trap doorway where you could see light on the other side. Meaning the light didn't shine into the room and illuminate anything, but when you looked out of the tiny door, you could see reality. For whatever reason, they needed to get to that place to be able to speak.

I got the sense that they were trapped in the room and didn't want to be there. This was consistent across all of the beings in there–they wanted out. The best analogy I have is that they were crackheads and someone had entered the room with a hit. They were fighting with each other and desperate to get a turn. Better yet, it was as if they were addicted to speaking and something about me entering gave them a chance to take a hit and speak.

The first few times I visited the room, I would just wake up after what felt like a night of sleep to find myself at the airport. I would be covered in sweat. Nothing happened that I could remember except the crackhead voices pushing me around, acting desperate.

But one time, a male voice came to me from above it all, and said, "Come with me."

I got to leave the dark room with this voice and for once in that altered state, I felt safe. The voice belonged to something that felt like an elder, it was saintly even. As if someone pure and wise had pulled me from a scathy crowd.

And he showed me everything. Stars, outer space, lifetimes. The entire universe. When you exit linear time, you can see it all at once and also one moment as it all–and both experiences are at the same time. There is no measure of moments or tangible way to explain how I absorbed the entire universe.

I would meet this voice again in future drug induced states on the mule plane, and in those meetings, I would ask to go back and see certain parts again. But he wouldn't always let me. He was in control of what we went back to. Flashes of memories, past and future for my human self, would be slowed down to experiences that I could re-enter.

One of these re-entries was my death as an advanced being. I understood it to be me, but it felt like the future. And I looked different. After experiencing this death, he told me that now I was ready. I could meet the creator.

He took me to a giant place. Like a colosseum of gaseous energy where we were all floating balls of light. And it was big enough to hold millions of us. There was a visual element to this experience, but not like looking through eyeballs. I could "see-sense" objects. The best way to explain what it means to "see-sense" is that I was aware of these objects, but they fall outside of the human perceivable spectrum using our five senses,

We were all in rows, waiting. And we waited for a very long time. Again, I have no way to measure this time, just that I experienced a great deal of waiting.

Then a voice said, "I'll see the ones that put themselves first."

These souls moved forward towards a massive whirling, black energy ball in the middle of the giant colosseum-like place. The only colors I remember perceiving were shades of deep black, shades of grey, and very little white. While we could all hear this voice, loudly, only this group seemed to be being addressed.

"Do you see what you've done?" the voice asked the ones that put themselves first.

"Now go and fix everything you've done."

There was cheering. I could hear conversations around me. They were happy because the ones that had moved forward were the ones that had victimized others.

And then we all waited for a very long time again.

Then the voice said, "To the ones that put others first, return. Make it better."

I could hear discussions around me about how this task was even harder. The ones that put themselves first had a specific fix, and they knew exactly what it was that they were to do. My group of souls felt that they needed to make everything better. We didn't know what would give us a "passing" mark, or if we might fail again. I remember knowing that I needed to revisit every lifetime and somehow make it better. The assignment felt so vague. I sensed that everyone was as confused as I was.

From that moment, I was whisked away. I woke up immediately. I was on a plane in Santa Marta, Colombia.

When I woke up in Colombia, I did not remember this experience, but I felt it.

In my normal life, I would begin to remember parts of the flights and specific memories in my teens long before my twenty year tour memories came back. Flashes, snippits even, especially the timer. I always remembered a timer; a countdown to doom.

CHAPTER 2

The Timer

There was another time I remembered the dark room, the voice I traveled with, and the timer. For some reason, growing up, I would get sick almost every Good Friday. It was the kind of sickness where I'd pass out on my bed and enter a deep, sweaty, sleep–a fever induced hallucination even. I would see visions and flashes of these scenes, but I was young and they didn't mean much to me. It's amazing to me how much we experience as children without giving oddities much thought or questioning.

I saw myself on a ship. It was a pod roughly the size of a car that was clear like glass. I was in space and I wasn't human. In this vision, I was a brown, skinny humanoid flying this glass pod. On the dashboard of the pod was a timer, counting down. I had the overwhelming sense of being late. There were voices coming in over my intercom telling me to hurry, I still had time to make it.

The timer was counting down from two measurements of time, but they weren't minutes. Time was different in this glass ship. One unit was the equivalent of roughly five minutes here.

The intercom was relentless, "Head back now. Turn back, you can still make it."

I was telling them there was something wrong with my ship, that I couldn't move out.

"We see nothing wrong with your ship. You need to engage and get out of there. Immediately."

At some point of the timer countdown, roughly two earth minutes, they stopped talking to me. They left me alone. And I felt relieved. It was stressful for me to tell them about my ship's malfunction. Because it was a lie. They stopped communicating with me when it was too late anyway.

When the timer got to zero, there was a bright flash of light and then I'd wake up. This whole scene was a recurring dream throughout my entire life.

I've had several other recurring visions. They're not as prominent and impactful as the timer, but they've been on repeat too. It can be difficult to recall things that fall outside of chronological order, because I believe there's a part of the brain that's activated when we can put things in order–maybe the part of the brain that is responsible for recall. Who knows. Regardless, I often saw flashes of my life, but I didn't realize at the time that they were me.

I would see myself standing on stage. I saw a girl walking away from me and then turning around and looking back at me. I feel an intense emotion not necessarily recognizable–the girl nor the emotion. I see myself in a crash, very badly injured, in something like a helicopter car. I'm laying there. Broken, dying, replaying my life in my mind.

I'm on this flight with somebody that I know, though I can't recognize them now. They've been successful because of my influence, and they tell me such. In fact, the success has allowed them to purchase such a craft. I am old and disabled, as if I've had a stroke. I walk with a cane and don't see or speak well.

I sense that we're in a field in Michigan, and in this crash we're both dying. I begin to worry about what the last word out of my mouth will be, so I start reciting my three daughters' names, on repeat. I am in a great deal of pain.

In my last moments, I felt that I had done everything I set out to do. I did it all. I finished it–reached all my goals. I keep telling myself, "At least I did it all. I finished it."

It is not my personal belief that this is how I will

actually die. It's my belief that there are many possible outcomes, infinite possibilities, and for some reason, some of us get to see glimpses of possible futures sometimes. But I know that I could kick the bucket tomorrow too.

On my way back from the twenty year program, when I was in the process of having my memories erased, I also got to see more possible outcomes of my life. Possible deaths. In every version of my future that I have published my first book, *Ceres Colony Cavalier,* I die happy.

For some reason, the book *Ceres Colony Cavalier* causes a pivot in my life. In all instances, that pivot leads to positive outcomes. And I tell myself that I couldn't have done it without her.

****

If you are given the opportunity to take a ride in a helicopter car-type machine, are you going to get in?

Yeah. Of course. Because my choice would be to not live in fear more than it would be to walk into my own death event. I could also not die. When I made the conscious decision to choose living free over living in a state of fear, my entire life changed for the better. So that's my daily motto, when I start to feel fear or consider making decisions from a place of fear, I tell myself, "I'm not afraid."

CHAPTER 3

The Place Between

I suspect I was put on an anesthetic version of ketamine during the flights. In my personal research of soldiers in Viet Nam, I discovered this. They used ketamine as a field anesthetic because they could operate without monitoring the heart rate like they would need to with other anesthetics. Soldiers, when administered this ketamine, would have visions of future battles. And they were accurate. I'm guessing that what they gave me was something along those lines.

One day a drug shipment was canceled. This meant that they had an "extra" dose of the drug, because I wouldn't be needing it on the flight. There was a man that ran the goldmine just outside of town that wanted to pay my handlers to have me put under in order to get information from me about where to find gold.

Manuel, my handler, told me that he didn't know if I could control what went on when I went under, but that I shouldn't tell the gold mine man anything because he had a lot of money and he could buy me. He was known to kill children. And if he took ownership of me, after he had taken what he wanted from me, he would kill me too.

It was a bit of a voyage to get to him. We had to take a barge and cross two rivers.

They administered the drug and I went under. All he wanted to know from me was where to find more gold. I told him that the gold was "everywhere the river turns." He was angered by my answer and told them that I was a waste of money.

On the trip back home, Manual told me that I'd done a good job.

As it turns out, gold was and is everywhere. Nowadays, the entire city is expanding like wildfire. And it's all one big gold mine. Fifty miles in each direction, just one big gold mine—from the gold mine we visited all the way back to the original town.

Manuel told me once that I spoke fluent Spanish when the drugs from the IV hit and I went under. He said that he talked to his dead grandmother too. At some point, word got around Puerto Tahuantinsuyo that I was a transmitter for these beings in the room. Manuel started bringing a notepad on the flight with questions from people in the town.

I remember that there were things we would describe as good and things we would describe as bad. But most of all, as a young child, what I remember most clearly is that it was scary. Before I would go under, I was terrified. I had no control of my life on either side of the experience.

I would pray that the voice that came and got me would be there, and that it would come quickly. Sometimes it wouldn't come at all. Other times it would come get me and we wouldn't do anything, but I was still relieved to be out of the dark room. Leaving the room was not something I could do on my own, I had to wait for the voice.

When my awareness left the room, my body was still used as a transmitter. The beings in the room would use my body to speak to Manuel on the plane. I had zero recollection of anything they said through my body when I would leave with the voice.

I have no sense of who or what the voice was, just that it was older. To be more accurate, it was a brighter thought form, or louder. I couldn't say now who or what it was, but it definitely felt familiar. Sometimes it would take me out of the room and leave me somewhat floating in space while it did something. I didn't mind this suspended wait, I was actually relieved to be there. After I'd been there enough times, I started to get snippets of information when I waited. They were flashes of visions that somehow pertained to my life and seemingly other's lives.

I believe that the black room is a place somewhere between being dead and being alive. Dead but not yet free. Free like I was when I left that room–but on a much greater scale. I got the sense that some spirits got to live outside of that room, and continue their growth process, but that the ones in the dark room were still there sorting out their sickness. Those spirits were stuck there and desperate to leave. Outside of the room was wonderful. I could see the cosmos–the universe– but without eyes. I was aware of everything or at least a much, much bigger reality.

I could describe it as time traveling too. The voice would insert me into blips of my life where sometimes I was a kid, sometimes an adult. I could see my incarnation process, and the process of choosing my life, but it was all fluid, and I would bounce in and out of these scenarios without attachment to the need to make sense of them. Or to chronologically order them. Because they all felt like me.

I saw myself between lives, before I incarnated. There was someone there asking me what I wanted to work on and helping me choose what was best for my next voyage. I would describe them as a counselor or principal. I would consider whether I wanted to be smart or athletic, tall or short, male or female. Etc. And this being was in charge of making it happen, but it seemed to decide what I could and could not be and do as well. This was also based on what was available. Meaning, I couldn't go into the NBA, because all those roles were already taken by others.

I would witness flashes of this process, and then I would bounce out, into another scene or experience.

This is a place that I think many earth bound people strive to get too. Everything I've heard from other people's experiences with deep focus states, taking Ayahuasca, out of body experiences, and even some of what I went through at Inyokern in the trauma based programming – it seems like everyone is getting to this same place. And people often report the same thing. They find themselves outside of the confinement of the physical world where they enter a realm of new freedom. In this place, they remember how they got here and reconnect to the bigger picture. Life starts to all make sense, even though it still feels hard at times. What is a decade or two of hardship if it means spiritual growth from an eternal perspective?

For myself personally, I understood or remembered why I chose certain lives and what I was meant to do there. It created a sense of urgency for this life. I believe that I have crammed in a lot of debt in this life that I need to repay quickly. I believe that my current life is occurring after the, "Go back and make it better."

****

Who do you think the nice voice was?

I think it's me. God. I don't know. It's something that prefers to remain anonymous. Archetypally, it feels like a referee, as if life is a game and one person is there to ensure the rules are being followed. They can pause the game and reset things. But I would say that there was a closer feeling, like the referee was an uncle or big brother figure.

At one point, I'm certain I asked, "Who are you?"

I never got an answer. Again, it prefers to remain anonymous.

Have you heard the voice since your time in Peru?

Yes, in Hawaii. I share about this in Chapter 5.

Why do you think you remember so much?

I think it was a perfect storm. And there's no one answer. I think many things contributed to my remembering. I was in love with a girl, so I wanted to remember. I had an MRI that did something to my brain. Or maybe I was supposed to remember in this incarnation. It could be all of them and it probably is.

And I had forced contact with my higher self, on a monthly basis for two years. My experience on those flights in Peru was a perversion of consciousness. I don't believe you're supposed to go to this place as often as I did. Most people work really hard to get there and have only one or just a handful of contact experiences in their life. But I did it monthly, on repeat for years.

I think that on the other side of timespace, there's a place of being alive and being dead, and that's where I went. I think people in deep meditation and perhaps on plant medicine go to the place I was taken to when I went outside the room. Or at least the same plane of existence.

I would witness experiences in flashes, and then the voice might bring me back to them later and I'd had a more clear vision of what was going on when I'd first seen the flash. This actually made me feel more lost, and left me with more questions. Seeing more and knowing more does not always provide the answer we think it will. Sometimes it makes it harder to understand.

Do you think going to this place is something you can train yourself to do?

I think probably. But if I did it now, I would see things from my adult self, as opposed to through the eyes of a child like back then.

I think kids can train themselves to go there. It gets harder when you're older. Kids are more of a blank canvas and adults are already painted, so there's only so much more you can add to the canvas.

A lot of Near Death Experiences I've watched describe experiences just as profound. They connect to higher information that puts their life in a completely different perspective.

Every time I went under, I came out with a new and different perspective. Even though Manuel and his boss would constantly tell me they would kill me if they needed to, when I woke up I knew I was safe because I'd seen my future.

I think Manuel always kept me at arms length, too, because he knew at some point, he might be ordered to kill me. I suspect that task would have been easier for him if he didn't care about me.

CHAPTER 4

The Kama-Loka &
The Bird Guide

When Tony told me of this dark room, it resonated with my personal experience. Not as a medium, but instead with my experiences working with plant medicine in Peru.

As a medium, I don't see anything like a dark waiting place between life and death. Instead, I would describe what I see in my connected state as souls traversing realms to manifest and visit with us in recognizable forms physically near our awareness. Or more specifically, my awareness. Which isn't saying much because I also believe our awareness is immeasurable and everywhere. I think all souls go to the same place after death and that they visit us through the same voyage process, that happens in a flash. To put it very simply, souls are here in an instance as soon as we're ready to connect. And mediums like myself can help with this connection.

This dark room that Tony describes reminds me of what the Hindi language calls the Kama-Loka, or the "desire place." It is an immaterial plane where disembodied personalities stay for an undefined amount of time after their human death. If they lived a life of service, they might stay a matter of days, or hours. But if they were consumed by their own ego or had an unnatural, early ending, such as someone who committed suicide, they could stay for decades. It is an uncomfortable place for a personality to reside as they are not bound to the body nor are they reconnected to source energy. It would make sense to me that someone trapped here would be desperate to be heard, or to get out. Much like the voices in the dark room Tony describes.

My personal experience with this dark place was during a ceremonial journey with the plant medicine Huachuma, a powerful mescaline I took in Peru. This was in April of 2018. I had originally traveled to Peru to take Ayahuasca, which is another ceremonial plant medicine that works by blocking the stomach's metabolism of DMT, a naturally occurring molecule that all of our bodies produce. There are two plants used in the Ayahuasca brew, the one that provides the beta-carbolines, allowing DMT to exist, and a second that contains additional DMT. In theory, you should have a roughly six hour hallucinogenic experience when you consume Ayahuasca.

I tried the Ayahuasca brew multiple nights in a row, doubling down on my dosage, with little to no effect. One night, I did see a purple bird light that spoke with me through my thoughts, but this experience was not of any greater impact than a deep meditation. On the night of my final attempt, I eventually left the group of others partaking in the ceremony to go back to my hut in the jungle. As I closed my eyes to sleep, astral projection was easy. I took a psychic scan of the jungle and saw that many races of non-human species were nearby.

When I asked the Shaman about my lack of experience, he asked me what I did for work. We were talking through a translator as this Shaman, Mateo, did not speak a word of English. In fact, he only came out of the jungle to lead ceremonies once a decade or so and even then, only because he had a deep love for our guide, Jerry Willis.

When I told Mateo that I am a medium and work with departed spirits, he waved his hand as if to blow me off entirely. Then he spoke with the translator, who told me that Mateo had said, "You are Ayahuasca." He shared that mediums work in the same realm that the plant medicine brings us to, and that I was already there frequently.

I felt kinda ripped off to be frank. I had spent thousands of dollars and days of travel to get there and be told I was the medicine I was seeking. But the next day, we were offered Huachuma, which was described as "light and pleasant".

I wanted to get my money's worth, so I immediately downed the medicine, hoping for a day of laughter with the others in my group. And the first four hours of the journey were just that. I have never laughed so hard in my entire life.

But then reality started to morph, or expand more accurately. I looked out on the Amazon river and saw pink dolphins. They would surface and splash, then retreat under the cloudy brown river water. Except when they retreated, I could see their energy bodies as a blue color through the water. I was following them and would tell people when and where they were about to resurface. I was losing my shit and my friends around me were bugged out by my predictions of surfacing, mostly because I was completely accurate.

It's worth noting that there are pink dolphins that live in the Amazon river.

I began to see an expanded range of colors. I could see

other people's energy bodies and where they had injuries, both physical and spiritual. To one friend on the trip with me, I exclaimed in shock that "She was a man."

She started crying and told me how incredibly mean that was. She was a very muscular woman, but that wasn't why I had said it. I could see people's hormones. And she was more male than female.

I had taken the Huachuma about an hour before most people in my group and I could feel that I was going further and further from where they were. I was making my friends cry and completely off my face at that point. I wanted to get away from the group. I climbed a ladder to a canopy above the treetops to be on my own for a bit. I thought that the medicine would soon wear off and I wanted to watch the sunset over the rainforest canopy, which to this day is one of the most beautiful I've ever seen.

As the sun set, I felt myself melt into existence, merge with my surroundings in the jungle. I felt tired. At perfect ease. I laid back in the hammock and closed my eyes. And then I entered the dark room.

I went from a place of complete oneness with nature to a place of dark chaos. It was beyond uncomfortable. I was absolutely desperate to get out of there, but I could not open my eyes. There were things coming for me, but I would not have described them as beings like Tony. They felt like experiences, emotions even, and terrible ones. Things we don't want to feel. Guilt, shame, condemnation. But I couldn't clearly understand any of it. Intensely chaotic is truly the best I could describe it.

And then a silence and a stillness fell over it all, and an aqua-violet, feathered being with a beak being cut through the realm as it came for me. I would describe this being as androgynous to slightly female, and it was wearing a type of cloak. Not human below the head, but human size and with odd hands and feet that I could not focus my vision on.

She felt safe. Like she knew the ropes in this realm. She made them even. But she also scared me because she carried the absolute essence of truth. And truth is powerful, confronting even. Something we all say we want. But most of us are full of shit.

"Are you ready to come with me?" she asked.

"To where?"

"To get what you came for," she laughed at me.

I would do anything to get out of that dark, intensely chaotic, room. But it also hurt to step towards her because I knew I had to leave my delusions behind.

And I loved my delusions. I didn't know it until that moment, but I was in love with all these little stories that I had created about myself and my life.

"Are you ready?" she pressed me.

"Ok," I said, and as I set my intention to move near her, I merged with her.

In no passing of time at all, not even a flash, I found myself in the kitchen of my stepmother's house. I was seven or eight years old. I was being abused and I was in a state of desperate terror. My stepmother used to make up things that I did not do, then force me to admit them to my father and get punished.

"Not this," I told the feathered guide,"Take me back now. I don't want this."

It was more uncomfortable than the dark room with the emotion laden entities. It was personal, and unlike the dark room, this felt like mine. This was not something I could convince myself had nothing to do with me. This was a memory of my real life, but I was living it, in real time. I was there.

"Get me out of here, now. Is this a sick game?"

"You cannot leave until you feel it."

"I don't want to feel this. I've spent my whole life trying not to feel these terrible things from my past."

"That's the point."

"I'm going to die. My heart is going into shock." I was frantic, my body gasping for air and weeping in the hammock.

"Get me the fuck out of here."

"I am here. And you are safe, but you have to feel all of this."

I took a deep breath, both in my physical body and in this suspended memory that I was revisiting. And then I let myself feel it all. Everything I had tried to run from for twenty-seven years. I don't know how long I was there. But I surrendered and I stayed.

"Good," she said.

And then I hit the floor like I'd been dropped from twelve feet in the air. But it wasn't the floor, it was my body—in the hammock. I opened my eyes to see the treetops. To say I was disoriented is an understatement. I was snotty, shaking both from the mescaline and from the nervous system overload of slamming back and forth between realms.

"What is real?" I asked myself.

I closed my eyes to weep, to comfort myself. But the moment I sealed out the light, I smashed back into the dark room.

And she was there, my bird guide, as were the emotion entities. Just waiting for me—fear, guilt, and shame. These disgusting parasites that weren't mine. They wanted to use my body as some kind of enhancement mechanism for their survival. They planned to take me over entirely. I had to decide between staying with them, or leaving with the truth. And following the truth hurt, bad. Probably just as bad as staying, but I knew the journey with my bird guide was going to transform me for the better.

She asked me if I was ready again, and I went with her. I followed this process of re-entering experiences from my life, feeling everything I was too scared or too weak to feel, then being dropped back into my body twice more. Each time passing through the dark room. Each time making a choice to leave the room.

Then the fourth time I closed my eyes, she met me in the absence. I say absence because it was not the room, but it was not anything. There was no setting, nothing to frame the experience by. We were just sounds in the great void.

She told me that I was to live my life with an open heart. That my job on earth was not to protect my heart the way I had been before we traveled together. Because I wasn't really protecting it, I was closing it off. And it was not broken, it was tired.

She clenched her fist tight, "This is your heart. Relax."

Then we morphed into a light shape and she showed me how the "sparrow's wings" are perfectly designed to fold nicely over the shape of an anatomical heart.

"I will guard your heart from this moment until forever. And if you will trust us, you can live free. In love, and free."

When she said "us" I knew there were many. Infinite more like her.

Something about Tony's description of the dark room felt familiar. And I often wonder if we were crossing the same place, but giving different descriptions. Because we are different people, with different vantage points and perspectives. He told me once that he also felt that the voices in his dark room wanted to project their negative states onto him.

I learned upon my return to New York City, where I was living at the time, that there is an acupuncture point at the base of the xiphoid process, or sternum, called

"Dovetail" because it looks like the tail of a bird, with the ribs on either side representing the bird's wings.

A few years after this experience in the Peruvian jungle, the friend that I had called a man told me that her testosterone was high and that it had been causing her health problems.

CHAPTER 5

The Cliff

I think it was around 2013 that I was living in Maui, Hawaii, working as a property manager for a man that owned fourteen or so properties on the islands. One of the properties was a one-hundred acre spread outside the town of Kahakuloa. There were two towering cliffs, between which a river ran through when we got heavy rainfall. It was a stunning place to me, and the owner agreed to let me camp there from time to time.

My wife and I set out one evening to camp overnight on one edge of the cliff. We had a wonderful evening under the stars. She left for work in her car the following morning and I decided to leave my truck near the campsite when I went to work on the property. My plan was to walk back to get my truck at the end of the day and drive home.

The campsite was on the opposite side of the valley from the property that I was maintaining. Instead of walking up and around like I had that morning, I decided to climb down into the valley and come back up on the other side, near our campsite and my truck. It was so beautiful in the valley–I wanted to explore. Plus I had never been in that valley before.

It was a lovely afternoon. I had a machete that I kept on my belt, which is common on the islands, to clear walking paths or overgrown vines and brush. I was hiking in my work boots.

I started walking down into the valley, where the composition of the dirt began to get more and more dry. At one point, the dirt gave way and I fell. I started sliding downward. Out of instinct, I grabbed my machete to try and stab it into the ground to stop my sliding. It worked, but it cut my hand in the process. On top of that, every time I tried to wiggle myself up, the blade would dislodge slightly and I would slip a little more.

I eventually slid down into a bush that I was able to grab ahold of. It was at this point that the machete dislodged completely and slid right past me. What I then heard was the machete clank down the cliff and eventually hit rock. It sounded like a terribly long fall. There was so much clanking before the final smack.

When I looked in the direction the machete had slid, I could not see the edge, but I did see treetops below me. I started to panic. Treetops means there was a twenty to thirty foot drop.

The bush that I was holding on to wasn't very big and the roots had begun snapping free from the dirt as I was hanging. There were large pieces of the rock and loose dirt beneath my flailing feet that were also breaking away each time I moved. I could hear them free fall to the ledge, then clank and smack stop in the same manner as my machete. It was then that I realized I was in deep shit.

I knew I was at the edge of the cliff and that I couldn't go back up. I didn't have the strength and the terrain was against any kind of ascent. I had been in parts of the valley before and I knew it was rocky at the bottom and there was no cell service. I considered falling off the edge and breaking my legs. I would not be able to call for help though. It's incredible how much information you can process and consider when you're in true danger. I was making peace with myself. I was about to die and I was coming to terms with this being the last moment of my life.

To make matters worse, red fire ants were coming from the uprooted bush onto my hands. I accepted there was nothing more for me to do. In the process of giving up, I heard a voice in my head. It sounded like the same person that used to come and get me out of the black room that I went to under the IV on the Peru flights. It asked one simple question.

"Don't you trust me?"

An immediate peace came over my body.

"I trust you."

Then not only did I let go, but I pushed off. I wasn't sure if I was pushing off because I was sure I was going to live, or because I was truly okay with the thought of dying. But I pushed off like a Nestlé plunge because more than anything, I trusted that voice.

I fell through a tree and then into cane grass. There were vines from the tree that tangled around me and absorbed my fall. When I came to a stop, I was about six inches above the ground in the cane grass, as if I was laying back in a recliner.

I was delighted to be alive. That's an understatement. But there aren't words for some feelings.

I had a few scratches from the cane grass and the cut from the machete on my hand, but I was otherwise unharmed. I looked to my side to find the white skeleton of a ram, with my machete lodged in its rib cage. It had been there for quite some time. I grabbed my machete and I cut myself out of the vines.

I hiked down to the ocean, through the most wonderful field of flowers, then back to my truck. I will never forget the beauty of the flowers. From there I drove home. Simply drove home.

The entire time I was processing what the fuck voice said that to me? I knew that something profound had just happened to me.

Only when I started planning this book did I realize that it might be the same entity looking out for me this whole time.

****

Why are you sharing this story?

Because this moment changed my life. It set the tone for everything that I've done ever since. Before this moment, I was making most of my decisions from a place of fear. It was as if I was trying to protect myself from calamity, but calamity always happened. Or another way to put it is that my problems weren't really my problems, but instead that the fear I had of them was my problem. From this moment on, I started to rely on trust.

I still don't know who or what that voice was, and I'm not alluding to any one thing. But for the context of this book, I'm sharing that many things happen with or from another realm. And in some ways I want to normalize this experience.

Also, the more I work with people, the more I look back at this moment. I realize that fear limits your growth. Frankly you can't fly if you don't leave the nest—if you don't conquer that initial fear. And I also acknowledge that "they" are pushing fear upon us. It is literally at the heart of most of the world's problems.

CHAPTER 6

The Hallway on Ceres

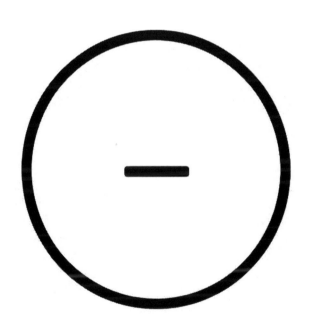

So, as promised, I'll tell you what happened in the hallway on Ceres.

I was a slave on Ceres for twelve years, plus roughly eleven years in this next extended dilation timeline that I'm about to explain.

On Ceres, we had weekends off for the most part. There was a random pool where we'd get assigned to do barrack duties on the weekend, like laundry and cafeteria work. I didn't get called in very often. One weekend evening, an officer came to the ladies at the window to call on me. They buzzed over the intercom in my room and told me to report to the front. There was a blonde man in a Ceres Colony military uniform waiting as I approached.

"Come with me," he said.

We took a short train ride to another connecting train and eventually ended up at an administrative type office. I was excited. I thought something good was about to happen to me. The officer was explaining to me that they had met a new group of advanced, grey extraterrestrials, and that a lucrative trade for technology had been struck. They needed manual labor and I was in the pool to go help. They were going to test me for the role and decide if I would qualify to be sent off.

I was apprehensive yet excited, thinking it would be a better position than what I currently had, which was monotonous work. We went through the administrative building, down a long hallway, where we came upon probably fifty other guys dressed just like me, all lined up in front of a set of double doors. I could hear someone screaming towards the end of the hallway, behind the two doors. Two men approached me and the officer and took some information down. The two guys that walked up were in light grey, casual uniforms. They were a part of the Ceres Colony base.

"He's going to be tested, right?" asked the officer who had escorted me there.

"No, they don't need testing. He's going."

Then my escorting officer left. I was instructed to simply wait in line and do as I was told. The screaming guy was brought out of the room and escorted another way, further from us. They were intentionally restraining him from interaction with the others in line. I was in line for another fifteen minutes or so. Three or four more guys went in, then another came out distressed, screaming and writhing from their restraint.

He was skinny, extremely distressed, and desperate to get the attention of the rest of us in line.

"Don't go. Don't go. It's more than ten years. KILL YOURSELVES!" he shouted as they hauled him off.

At that point, two armed guards came out and told us that we were to remain in complete silence. Otherwise, we'd be shot. They moved the line back even more so that when new guys came out from the room, they could be shoved off without passing or interacting with anyone in line.

When it was my turn to enter the room, I walked onto an inclined table. There were two grey extraterrestrials of a race that I'd never seen before. They had wider heads than I'd ever seen and were a much darker shade of grey.

I was strapped onto the table and told that I was going to be serving another ten year term.

"You can't do this. It's illegal. I've been told it will make me go crazy."

"That's not true," an officer in medical gear responded.

"This is completely different technology and you'll be fine. You'll be right back."

Then I was immediately stuck with a needle in the back of my neck, and another into the tear duct of my right eye. I did go for ten years, a little more actually, and I could have been there for much longer. Hundreds of years even. Because the devil steals.

I woke to find myself extremely disoriented, in a small outer-spacey looking room with metal walls and a metal, bunk-type bed. The floors seemed to be made of some kind of polished stone. It was the size of what I imagine the average prison cell to be. But this place was nicer than a traditional cinder block prison cell.

I started searching around the room. I don't even know what I was looking for really. Maybe light switches? An exit? Some kind of link to normalcy, except that I had no memory of anything before that moment – so I can't say exactly what I was hoping to find or figure out. I had this notion that I could find a brochure or something to explain what was going on, but there was nothing. There was a door, but it was locked. I was completely alone with no sense of what existed outside of this room.

The most similar experience I could compare this to would be coming out of a drunken black-out. Where you know you got there somehow, but you're completely disoriented and have no idea how you got there. Except add the element of a new physical form in a completely new environment.

There was a flat screen television-type device at the foot of the bed, mounted to the wall. It had a few options on it, like an interface, where you could choose what to do. Not far from the other end of the bunk, there was a doorway that went into the bathroom, which was very small. It had a weird, oddly shaped toilet. Our toilets on earth are oval-shaped. This was more of an oblong octagon, with squared edges and made of metal. There was no water for the flush. You just put the lid down and it was an automated process.

There was also what you might call a stand-up shower, but without water. I would later learn that the "shower" was actually ultrasonic and utilized a form of light that would sterilize your body. If you had dirt on you, it would essentially shake off. There was a form of grating at the bottom of the shower where the dust particles would fall through.

There was a mirror. It was about the size of a small baking sheet. I saw myself as clearly developed, meaning I had grown into this body but at the same time, I'd never seen myself before. I had the feeling that I had been something different before, but I didn't know what.

I was not a human. I was a brownish-tan alien with three long fingers and a long thumb. I was skinny, with no hair, and had an interface port on the back of my neck, right at the base of my head. I had a skeletal structure, much like a human body. I was roughly five feet tall.

My eyes were like human eyes, with a pupil and a grey surface similar to the whites of human eyes. I had a long skinny nose that was very small. There were two nostrils that were mostly inadequate. I had a sense of smell, but it was faint. I did not have ears, but more of a pronounced ridge where ears would normally be. My skin felt dry and cracky, like the skin on the bottom of an unmanicured foot. And it had an itchy essence to it like dry human skin would.

I was wearing a one-piece jumpsuit with a zipper along the entire left side. The jumpsuit was greyish and I was also wearing blue socks. I was discovering all of these things about myself and it felt so foreign. Again, I felt like someone was going to need to explain all of this to me.

I don't remember bleeding during my time as this being. But I do remember bruising and when I did, the bruises appeared black in color. I did have a few medical tests, where they drew blood and it was in the red family, but very dark. Like a deep plum-wine color.

I had a port on the back of my head, just above my neck, that was about the same diameter as a pen. I was soon to learn that the port took a quarter twist to lock in a cable when I connected. This was a sort of docking station for connection to a virtual interface so realistic that when I reflect back, I can't always tell what I was seeing in reality and what I was seeing through the interface. It took over my senses completely.

I found a remote control device in my room and worked out how to turn on the flatscreen television looking thing. A screen popped up with a menu that was not in english, but I could read it. On the screen was a map, a schedule, a locked option called "Entertainment", and messages. I tried to click on the messages option, but there was nothing there. Every option I tried was blank or locked out.

I felt anxious to do something, anything, and also extremely defeated. I laid back on the bed and fell asleep. I woke up sometime later, mad. Really mad. I started hitting things–throwing a fit.

The television came on and instructed me to stop and to stay calm. It wasn't English, but it was a language that I could understand. I hit the television again, and this time a light and sound came on. The light was reddish in color and the sound was almost supersonic. And it hurt. It irritated my entire body. It was maddening. It was most similar to salt water on fresh shaved skin, with an added element of heat. It wasn't high intensity pain, it wasn't actually what I would even consider pain, but it was unbearable nonetheless. The voice told me to remain calm, or that I would be corrected again. I responded that I wanted to talk to someone. I needed to know what I was and what I was doing there. No one answered my demand for answers.

I sat down, in complete despair. I waited–for what I don't know–and then I fell asleep again. I awoke to the screen telling me to get up and get ready. It told me how to use the shower and where to find my new clothes. There was a drawer that pulled out from under my bed where I could find what I needed to get dressed.

I had different teeth, they were larger and I had less of them, and they did not need brushing. They were more like long ridges than teeth. I didn't know it then, but the food we were given was also formulated to clean our mouths when we ate.

I sat, cleaned and dressed, for what felt like four hours. Then my door unclicked and the screen alerted me that I could exit and that I was to report to my post.

Outside of my door, I discovered a long hallway with walls of stone, like smoothed mountain rocks. There were sporadic windows, which was odd, because it was pitch black outside of them. There were also screens along the hallway. If I looked to the left, it was just a long hallway with no end in sight. There was bright lighting all along the hallway that I would describe as glossy. It made everything shine. To my right, there was an end in sight and more individuals like me–twenty or thirty of them standing around a screen. This was what I presumed to be my post. I walked towards the group of individuals like me so I could ask them what was going on.

CHAPTER 7

John

The second most common question I get asked about from the first book, *Ceres Colony Cavalier,* is about the black kid from the moon.

I had the opportunity to volunteer for high risk missions in hopes of being awarded a promotion for our efforts during my time as a slave on Ceres. One of the high risk missions I went on involved a stop-over on the moon.

After landing on the moon, I was led through an umbilical unit by two officers. One turned to me. "Do you know where we are? We are on the moon," he advised me. "You're lucky to even be here, most people that come here, never even get to be at this level. We are on a deeper level—a top secret area of the moon. And just because you're not wearing our uniform, that doesn't mean you're gonna take any shit from anyone because you're from Ceres Colony. We are the best there is. Best of the best. Take shit from nobody. Don't forget that."

It was actually called Ceres Kolonie Gesellschaft, not Ceres Colony Corporation, the way I often refer to it in english. I think Gesellschaft translates loosely more as "organized society" than corporation, but most everything was "Corporation" out there.

The two officers were pumped and drilled me with this rhetoric.

"You're no slave today," the other said over his shoulder. "You're Ceres Colony Corporation Personnel, and all these people here need to show you respect. You need to walk like it."

The other one seemed like he was selling me something. Trying to pump me up.

"Zero Hour is here! We are Mittenachtwoffe!—The first to travel space other than these American fuckers!"

I felt that they were both a little too exuberant. I tried to get in the spirit though, thinking that maybe this frame of mind is what it takes to get promoted. One gave me a pen-like device.

"Here," he said, thrusting it in my hand. "You'll need this. It's your translation device. With this, you can understand any language being spoken on the Moon."

We eventually made it through the winding hallways to a checkpoint supervised by grey aliens. The same species I'd encountered on the moon before. Condescending and cold. The officers were handed some paperwork they needed to fill out at a nearby window.

"Wait here," they said, lowly.

Upon their return, we went through a door and began our journey along several more very tight hallways with different colored lines on the walls. As we turned corners, we came across several other ET species that were walking the hallways. There were humanoid ones that looked like us but with elongated heads and longer faces, a little taller. That and more greys. There were also humans in one piece uniforms, akin to a jumpsuit. My surprise was obvious to the officers.

"Don't look so impressed—even if they are an advanced race of species—you're from Ceres Colony. You are representing the finest colony of this Solar System."

To be clear, I was receiving their commands through the translator. They were speaking the same dialect of German that everyone spoke on Ceres. These guys must've had years of confidence boosting morale, and I'm not going to lie, it felt really good to be amongst them. I had such low self esteem, it really did make me feel valued and important for a change. Upon learning of this mission, I had mentally prepared myself for death. So any type of life threatening situation that would come across my path on this mission, I would not avoid, as I felt it was my ticket out of this damned life. I had been so miserable for so long, this was exactly what I needed to hear from these young, shiny Ceres Officers. It definitely stroked my ego, and it was the first time to even remotely hear this kind of talk.

As we turned another corner, the Ceres officers got sidetracked by someone and stopped to talk. In my distraction however, I kept walking a little farther ahead. Around the next hallway corner, I noticed a young black boy being escorted by two greys. And these weren't the typical greys. They were much skinnier and darker in skin tone than any I had seen up until that time. This young boy, no more than eight years old, was in a medical gown and had tubes sticking out of his body. There were bandages, predominantly on his head. It was as if he had just come out of surgery. He was being extremely uncooperative with the greys.

The boy saw me and made eye contact with me. Within an instant, he came screaming at me "Ahhhhh!!!" with his arms stretched out as if to hug me.

In a knee jerk reaction, I put my foot up to stop him and he bounced off my foot onto the ground. I'd caught him square in the chest and it was clear I had knocked the wind out of him. It was like I delivered a kick, and he also ran full into the kick. It wasn't until I saw him start to cry on the ground that I recognized the disappointment. His eyes told me that he wanted a hug, to be loved, or comforted. He was a child seeking nurture from another human being.

I felt crushed. The two greys approached quickly and motioned for me to stand back.

"What happened?" one of the Ceres officers demanded, running up to me.

They then looked at the greys who were busily injecting the boy with something to sedate him.

"What happened? Is there a problem?"

"No—no problem," the greys shook their heads quickly.

"Please do not raise this as an issue. He is unruly. We are sorry for any trouble he has caused," we all heard them say to us telepathically.

I watched the greys stand him up and stare at him for a moment. He stopped crying and looked hypnotized. Then they guided him with a hand on his shoulder back to where he had started running from. The three of them disappeared inside a door off the hallway. This would be an important event and memory for me years later on earth, post recall, because this young boy and I found each other in

2016 or 2017 on Earth.

He found me through one of my interviews and connected with me through an online social platform. He had watched one of my very early interviews and recognized me. He had heard the story of visiting the moon. While I've shared the scene above in both books now, I had not, at that time, shared this event.

When we finally connected, he told me that he was mad at me for years after the hallway and that he had wanted to kill me. I was taken back by this and assumed he was crazy.

I get a lot of messages from people who claim to know me or that they were this or that person in my story. I admittedly get too used to brushing claims like this off. But some part of me still wanted to give him a chance, so I went for it. I asked him what had happened then.

He said he was from the moon and that what I did was a "dick move."

"I hated you after that," he told me, casually.

From my perspective, he had run towards me with arms wide open to hug me and in return, I kicked him. It was that simple. I had been talked up to be something I wasn't and I wanted to look tough. So I had just lifted my leg, but he was a little boy and it hit him dead in the chest and he fell down. Then they took him back to where they were headed.

For a few minutes, I felt tough. Like I was somebody cool. But not long after, I felt guilt. It was the wrong thing to do. And I always wondered what happened to him. He was so desperate, crying, and pleading to not go. He was clearly suffering–pleading to not participate in what they were doing to him anymore.

When we spoke on the phone, he told me what they were doing with him. They were chemically and physically altering him to psychically track down targets and kill them. He would go to other worlds and either psychically kill them or physically kill them. Especially the ones that were weaker than he was.

They were putting him into dark rooms with hybrid animals that psychically attacked him over and over. He was being trained to psychically protect himself or fight back.

He was young and drugged, so the way he remembered things was altered in my opinion.

He said that when saw me, he could see that I was human because of my aura. I was the only one in the scene that had an aura and he knew that he could be safe with me. He was, at the time of seeing me, in the middle of a specific treatment where he could clearly see auras. And all he wanted was a hug.

****

What's such a big deal about him for you?

Many people reach out to me and say they knew me. John was different because he was the first one that reached out and said he remembered me. I was early in remembering and this had an impact on me. He was one of the accurate witnesses to my testimony. His memory was crystal clear and specific. It was undoubtedly the same incident.

Also, I was able to apologize to him. And that meant alot to me.

He did come out and share about his experiences in the programs in a limited number of interviews. But he was quickly ridiculed and his personal life was impacted. He has since gone silent on the topic. While this is kind of a shame, I understand why he did this.

Did you meet many black people or people of color?

Many, no. Several, yes. On the way back from that same mission, in that same hallway, I actually asked why there weren't black people in Ceres Colony to do the labor. They told me it was because it required a totally different system of mind control training. Black people specifically tended to break the programming and relapse into pre-training mode. They have a different will power where the programming wouldn't take. As far as I can remember, all other human races had the same training. But black people needed a completely different method of mind control.

For this reason, they tended to keep them all together in colonies that were at the edge of the solar system. And in these colonies, there were only black people because they could keep one infrastructure only for mind control, as opposed to needing several for each race of human slave. I believe they were doing hard labor like mining.

There was one other black person I had the opportunity to speak with, and he was on the ride back to the moon just before my return to Earth. He said he'd be moving a shovel for twenty-years, doing manual labor and lifting heavy things.

CHAPTER 8

Jackie's Experience with John

If this were really happening, we would know about it. More people would talk about it."

This statement kind of turns my stomach. Because nothing could be further from the truth.

I think it's more that *because* this is really happening, most people do not know about it. In fact, many digital platforms go through extreme, if not illegal, measures to keep this content from getting to the public. Or to distract the mainstream with headlines about one person slapping another at an award show while behind the headline scenes, bills are passed and lies are covered.

And people come out with the truth, like John, and their lives are turned upside down. They are shamed, ridiculed, banished in a way even. Families disown. Jobs fire. Friend's distance. Relationships leave.

So no, not really. I don't think it's really true that more people would know about this if it "were happening."

Plus it's not exactly coffee table chat, "Hey I was taken as a child and spent time on the moon, which is actually where most of the surgical augmentations go down."

Tony connected me with John after I shared memories of virtual reality training so real that you didn't know it was only in your mind until the visor came off.

He said there was another guy that talked about things the way I was sharing and showed me where to find him on Instagram. After some messaging back and forth, this guy agreed to Facetime with me.

We talked for several hours. When I saw his face, I told him that I knew him, but not as his Earth name. I knew him as John.

"Yeah," he told me, "that's what they called me out there."

And ever since, Tony and I have referred to him as John. To protect his privacy.

John told me the story with Tony slightly differently. He told me that he was with robots. That they were all robots and that Tony was the only human he had seen in a long time.

We shared mutual memories of training that we'd endured; levitating, practicing psychic connections with animals, and especially about the virtual technology so real you didn't know it was only in your thoughts. We were both fascinated by the ability this technology had to sync minds, meaning you and a teammate could be having the same, collaborative experience that overlapped just like reality.

Then he asked if I still had any of my skills. I told him that I wasn't sure if it was from my time in programs or just the way I was born as a human, but that I was a medium. We connected with his deceased grandmother, which was really special for me. She was a skinny, strong woman with a very particular wig. And she loved him dearly. I was affected by knowing he was so deeply loved.

He said he still had some of his skills. He could see things from other people's lives. He told me at some point in my life I would remember the "triangle headed beings" from the hallway of my childhood home. I have not yet, but that statement sticks with me too.

Then he showed me his artwork. There was one piece

in particular that moved me. It was massive–a canvas of blackness with blurred strokes of many colors.

"I like this one," I told him, "It feels familiar."

"Those are all people. Like faces. Or identities, kinda. That's what it's like out there," he responded.

CHAPTER 9

Training

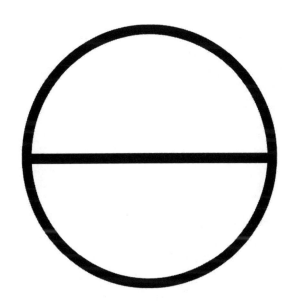

I was awkward with the group. It was like walking up to a class when a teacher was already teaching. I wasn't sure how they would receive me and I felt like I was interrupting, so I stood silently for quite some time. Inside, all could think about was asking someone what the fuck was going on.

We spoke through telepathy and verbal sounds but I wasn't good at telepathy yet. When I did speak, it was a different language altogether. To me, it sounded phonetically similar to the vowels and consonants of American English. I don't remember exactly what I actually said when I did finally speak, but it was something along the lines of asking if we were going to be told what we were all doing there. The members of the group were dismissive of me. They ignored me. I felt the same feeling as if I'd spoken up in a classroom and not only did the other students ignore me, but so did the teacher. I got the sense that most of them had been there for a bit. I later learned that new people came and went all the time, so they got used to entrances like mine.

When people ask me about the language we used, it really forces me to consider my memories–wouldn't I recall them, think about them even, in the language we spoke? Ultimately, I don't believe that we think in any language at all. I think our brain processes symbols, feelings, concepts even.

It's why we can't articulate some thoughts. And how babies can "think" about things pre-language acquisition. It's also how we can deeply understand complicated concepts that we cannot explain with words, and when we try to explain them, our knowingness of them seems to disappear as well.

Back to the group. There was one being that was taller and a grey color, explaining rules and showing a schematic of a ship on something that looked most similar to a map at the mall. It was a large, interactive screen that came up from the floor. Then the taller being handed out a piece of plastic with notes on it– it was rules for newcomers about how to behave really. It informed us on how to salute people, how to respond when Commanders and Officers entered a room or approached a group, as well as how to interact with each other. It also told us where we were allowed to walk and what would happen if we didn't, which was reassignment to a more difficult position.

I learned that this taller being was a commander. He looked identical to us, but was best described as what we humans would call a different race. All of the commanders had lighter, greyish skin and were taller, but were otherwise pretty similar. For the next ten years of my life, I never saw any other species than us–the tall and the short races.

This group of talls and shorts that I was a part of called themselves an acronym that I cannot remember. It ended with a word most similar to the english word Bureau, so that's what I'll call our group from this point forward.

From the meeting point, my group walked to a classroom where we watched a teacher using a giant video screen. The members of the group were catty with each other. Not necessarily rude, but we were immature. The classroom was boring. But I learned that we were on an asteroid, which seemed small compared to what we were learning about our project and what we would be doing. We were a speck in the sky compared to the scope of the project landscape. The Bureau was a corporation that built macro objects in space like planets, rings around stars, stars, and entire regions in space. Our crew was going to be contributing to the construction of a star. That I was aware of, there were six or seven thousand of us on this asteroid, and more than a trillion of us in this galaxy. At least that's what they claimed. There were other species in this galaxy, but we were the majority. And the entire galaxy operated under the same social structure.

The teacher was showing us how to use an interface through the plug into the back of our heads. Doing this would give us complete immersion in both our lessons and also when we got to our real "assignments". When I connected, I saw the same display as the screen, but this time in my thoughts. I was beyond creeped out by it and unplugged within seconds.

We continued to class for the next few weeks where we learned about our ships and what we would be doing. We'd meet at the same shopping-center map looking point where we'd get our first briefing and assessment of the day. From there, we'd be sent to different training areas or classrooms as some of us were more capable than others or at higher learning levels.

We were simultaneously watching flight training on a screen in front of us, and connecting the port in the back of our heads to a technology that allowed us to practice flight simulations. I got used to using the technology pretty quickly. But for some reason the task of plugging in was something I never did get used to. It was hard to find the hole but even more than that, it felt unnatural to stick something into my head. It was as if I had some subtle memory of being human–and connecting a machine to my brain, to my thoughts even, was beyond uncomfortable.

All of us were androgynous. We had no sex organs that I was aware of, at least not externally, and we excreted through one hole. Birds and reptiles have the same hole, called a cloaca. It's the end of both the digestive and reproductive tracts. The tracts separate internally, but they lead to one external hole.

I had the equivalent of what I would call reproductive energy, without knowing what it was. This resulted in restlessness with no release, that I could not understand. I asked for drugs or something to help me sleep at some point but was told no, that I was fine.

When I think back about my mental state, it was as if I was thirteen to fourteen years old. We all thought and acted like that–like adolescent boys. I suspect I was cloned, or engineered, because my mentality never advanced like it would have in a human body. Meaning, I stayed thirteen for the entire ten years. But the Commanders did seem to age mentally and had more of an adult, mature thought process.

I was intensely restless and got angry often. As soon as I did, I would get the light. In the early days of my time there, my room door was unlocked and I would get to walk around. It was just the simple, mostly empty hallway and I was always afraid to go too far. There was the mission board that I would walk to see but over time, that got boring. After a while, the door immediately locked when I went in anyway.

All of my time was spent either in the classroom or in my room. The bed in my room was a full size bed, and had a basic mattress built into the wall with the drawers where I found my clothes underneath. The drawers must have been connected to an internal hallway or some assembly line where our clothes were serviced. Meaning I would wake up to a fresh, clean, folded bodysuit each day. On the bed was a sheet and a thick blanket. I was trained to make my bed each morning before reporting to duty and once a week or so, I had to leave my bedding in a bag so that it could be washed. The screen in my room instructed me when to do these sorts of things.

There were lights that simulated daylight and darkness so we had some sense of a cycle. The "daytime" lights were like floodlights lined up underneath every window in the hallways. I had my own light switch in my room and would turn off the lights to sleep. There was an additional light in my room that must have had a sensor because when I stood up, it dimly lit the space. I didn't sleep well. I had dreams, but they were basic, lame dreams. Except for once, toward the end of my time on the asteroid. I dreamt of time running out.

If humans are 55-60% water, this body was more like 45% water. I would never sweat, and as I discovered my first day of waking up there, we didn't use water to shower. When we went to the bathroom, there wasn't a strong odor and it had a toothpaste consistency with occasional small amounts of liquid, not unlike bird droppings.

We also did not drink water. We could eat whenever we felt like it by pressing a button to dispense a serving through a drawer in our rooms. Our food was the shape of a Smartie but the size of a hockey puck, tasted like citrus, and came in three different colors. There was a dark one, an orange one, and a green one. It was a little thicker than pudding, like the consistency of pumpkin pie.

We would sometimes spend eight hours on our ships without using the toilet or eating food. Our biology was very different from that of Earth-humans, without the same biological needs or constraints.

So day-in and day-out, we kept to the same boring routine. Classroom, bedroom. Classroom, bedroom. Then one day we were told that we were finally trained and prepared enough to transition from flight simulations to flying our real ships. This was indescribably exciting. For starters, it was something new to add to the mundane routine. But even more thrilling was that we had been built up to feel confident about flying solo—even though for me, it was a terrifying thought.

We started in class with a quick briefing, and then were promptly marched to a hangar. At the hangar, each of us boarded an individual ship, which looked like a glass ball. We went in through the back, took our seat, and connected the ports in the back of our heads. It was a tight squeeze inside the ship.

Once our ports connected, we saw an interface inside the ship that illuminated an otherwise mostly dark experience. Each of the balls was lowered by a hydraulic lift to a bottom level where we were docked into a fuselage that sat at the rear of another black, square shaped ship. It was thirty to forty feet long and docked about twenty of us in the glass balls. I didn't see very much of this part of the departure, but I could hear everything. Once we were all secured in the fuselage, the floor above us would seal and everything would pressurize. Then a large door would open to space.

Our asteroid was in a nebula that made the space

around us completely black. The nebula was massive–light years massive. There were no stars, no atmosphere, just a vacuum. When we took off, there were lights off the base of the asteroid which allowed you to see our dimly lit base. The asteroid was shaped like a hamburger and I would estimate it to have been roughly fifty miles in diameter. There were buildings protruding off the asteroid and when we departed, we could see faint, blurry lights from the buildings. They were actually bright, yellowish flood lights, but the light did not travel far. The buildings were black and multi-storied, with windows, which made little sense given the range of visibility in the opacity of the vacuum. The buildings gave me the sense that there were thousands of others like me that lived on this particular rock in the sky. I'm not sure because I was never allowed to leave my area. I was permitted to go to my bedroom, the classroom, and the hangar. If I strayed outside of my allowed area of access, the irritating light would come on. But the Bureau felt like a massive, working corporate project, and we were just one small branch.

Our pods were released from the dock and we were off for our first flight out. The asteroid buildings and even the dock had artificial gravity. But when we were released, we experienced the drop to zero gravity. It was like going off a cliff without any altitude change. You had to mentally prepare yourself for the roller coaster feeling. If not, you would get dizzy, sick even. You had to mentally dive into the zero gravity.

At first, our flight path was mandated by a computerized control, which was remote from the Commanders in the tower. But soon, they released control to each of us. We took a slow lap around the asteroid. Time was measured in different units there, but it felt like about a twenty minute flight.

Roughly three of our minutes were equal to one of their time units. Similar to having sixty-minutes in an hour, they had twenty of these units in their secondary time unit. And the full "day" consisted of roughly twenty of these secondary time measurement units, like our twenty-four hour day. But there was no sun coming up and down–although it was simulated with the lighting–to mark any kind of planetary cycle like we experience on earth. Their "day" must have been based on the time we could work and the time we needed to sleep. Although I do recall being out on missions and feeling like we were called back early–that I could have worked for longer.

The purpose of our mission on this day was simply to get acquainted with the craft. I did not use controls, but instead navigated my craft with my thoughts, through the connected port.

We traveled together, in formation, a process that was also automated. The control team could set waypoints on our flight and I could switch to autopilot, but I could also turn this feature off at any point. Once we'd made our lap around the asteroid, we queued up by the hangar door and waited to be called one-by-one to dock. There was a crew of beings that looked like me waiting to service my craft upon return. They came and let me out and took over from there. My guess is that they were a sort of pit crew that prepped the pods for the next flight crew and moved them to the departure dock. We did not return to the same place from which we'd left.

After this short flight, I went back to my room where the screen menu was open. There were two new options–and they were games! At first, I just used the remote to click around and thought it looked really cool but I was too tired to engage. I decided instead to take a nap. When I woke up I plugged in and checked it out.

There were two single player games available and I could also see that there were more games that hadn't been unlocked yet. It was intuitive to me that the more I flew, the more games I could get. I had graduated in some way, and these games were a part of my new realm of freedom. They were the dangling carrot - I knew that the unblocked games were going to be my prize if I kept it up with my training and my flight missions.

Because I had the mind of an adolescent, this was incentivizing to me. And they were very basic games, like puzzle games or tetris, that truthfully only entertained me for fifteen minutes or so– but it was something to do.

It was through the video games that I learned that there were many citizens. We could interact with each other through short phrases, which were limited to a few words, but over time we could put a lot together. Some people were free. Some people were working in a military type role, some seemed to be in a position like me, and then there seemed to be others that were there at leisure. Some would talk about traveling and living in space and visiting planets on holidays.

I thought it was odd that someone who was free would come into these lame games, but they explained that they were there for the social component. This was the only way they could connect to some of their friends. But they had access to other, more advanced programs as well. They were more just popping in.

I think video games are pacifiers. Out there and here on Earth too. There are kids now that would rather play a video game than go out and socialize. They're also dangerous because they trick kids into thinking they've succeeded. It gives a false sense of self and accomplishment.

For us, the games gave us a false sense of freedom. When we were in the game, we believed we had freedom. They also act as a form of mind control where self perception is altered. They created scenarios where you became accustomed to being told what to do. This act alone limits original thought. You accept going by the rules, following the crowds, and being rewarded for following the plan. But still, the games were a welcome distraction.

I dressed the next morning to find that the symbol on the left arm of my jumpsuit was different. We all had a silver symbol on our jumpsuits and today, the circle was in a different placement. It was as if I had graduated a level. All of the Command had gold patches and our's, the flight crew, were all silver.

When we got back to class, everyone was talking about the games. Some people loved them. They were just okay for me. But eventually, they became my life. I got really good at them because that was all I had outside of the class room and our flight missions. People probably want to know about my day-to-day life in this place where I spent ten years, but this was it. Video games, my room, and my flight missions.

CHAPTER 10

The Mission

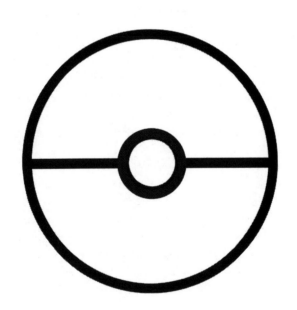

We didn't fly the next day, just took more classes. We got a report back from someone with a gold patch that we were dangerous and didn't know what we were doing. So we went back to training, with a simulator. It was a close experience to the flight, but without movement sensations and in the simulator, we had the feeling of gravity–plus there was no real danger. While much of our first real flight was automated, we still ran the risk of colliding with each other or even worse, with objects in space.

At first, we were tasked with simple point A to point B flights in the simulators. We made simple turns on a virtual course. Then we learned how to use two arms that came out of the bottom of our craft. There was also a device on the craft that could push objects in place–like a propulsor. They were training us to look for boulders in space the size of houses. We had to be able to select the good ones, the ones that were the heaviest elements.

We learned that our job would be to use our propulsor to push these space rocks into a giant gravity well. These rocks showed up as targets on our screens, not unlike a video game. Once we selected a rock, we were supposed to push it into the gravity well that looked like a giant purple ball in space on the screen. The gravity well was roughly three hundred and fifty thousand miles away from where we were working to push the mass.

From the asteroid where we lived to this work area, I would estimate it was a two hundred million mile journey. The reason I can estimate this is that our ships moved at 2AU an hour and it took us about forty-five minutes to get there. But again, we operated on a different unit of time.

So we had to find these certain space rocks, then we had to push these rocks up to a certain speed with our craft, and then we let go. The rocks were the size of houses, some of them were even the size of buildings–they were absolutely massive. Which is a funny thing to recall, as I would not have had any kind of reference to objects like a house or a traditional Earth building. This is an example of an instance where I don't know how I know, but I just know.

We would lock onto the rocks then get going up to speed, sometimes for two or three minutes before we released them towards the target. Once we push released them, the rocks would travel by momentum into the gravity wells. And it was possible to miss the well. We could do our best to propel them in the direction of the target, but sometimes it was a miss. We were far enough away that the rocks could encounter other objects on the way to the target. This would cause them to break apart at times. They would still hit the well, but not in the dead center where Command wanted the largest rocks. Command kept a score on our accuracy, which is how we knew when we missed.

They could also see when we pushed the wrong material forward. We would get a low "score" when we missed or threw the wrong material, which actually equated to nothing except being treated poorly sometimes. We didn't get any true punishment, but we did get a small reward for being accurate. They would release the equivalent of endorphins into the pleasure center of our brain and we would experience a brief mental stimulation.

The gravity wells were essentially a complex system of piled rocks and gasses that had been launched into place for hundreds of years, which was how long they'd been working on this project. Altogether, it was much larger than Jupiter. There was a science to where we threw the rocks, too. They wanted the biggest ones going directly into the center. For this particular training simulation time, we were scoping out the largest rocks and testing their elemental makeup. Command also sometimes instructed where to throw certain elements, which went into different layers of the process, following a very intentional plan for the star.

So we practiced rock hunting, testing elements, planning our target, and propelling them forward through the simulation training for many weeks, and in return, got seven or eight more games. And a new patch.

CHAPTER 11

Buster

When I was a kid on earth, around age seven, I had a special experience with an animal–a dog. My mom was out front of our house doing yard work and I was playing beside her. She was pruning the lilac bushes, which had just started blooming. Scent is strongly tied to memory, because the part of the brain that processes both is the same. The scent of lilac elicits memories of my childhood to this very day.

My sister was not far from me. The sky was overcast but it was pleasant outside and there was otherwise nothing too special about the day.

I remember the clouds clearing and the warmth of

the sunlight breaking through. My mom had us move to a shaded area under a tree and told us to wait there while she went to get some lemonade. At the same time, my dad arrived home from work. I think this particular moment has stayed with me because it felt perfect. Everyone was so happy.

My mom came back with a blanket, snacks, and lemonade. My sister and father got up to work on something together. It was just me on the blanket as my mom had also gotten up at that point to get back to her yard work. All of the sudden, a furry, black, mutt looking dog came running at me full speed. It jumped into my arms and started licking me all over my face. I can still feel the emotion of the moment–every part of the equation was perfect. It was everything I needed as a child to feel unconditional happiness. And feelings like this stick with you.

My sister rushed over to check it out. The dog interacted with her for a moment, but then it came straight back to me. Like we had catching up to do. We discovered that the dog was a boy and he did not leave my side for the rest of the day. When I went inside, he stayed on our porch and waited for me. My dad would not let us take him inside. He believed that this dog must have come from a neighboring property and that we needed to let him go back home. This didn't make sense to me as a child because we knew all the neighbors within three miles and none of them owned this dog. He must have come from very far.

But he never left. For days he waited for me to come outside with him. I begged my dad relentlessly to make him ours. I cried multiple times pleading my case. My sister loved him too and joined my effort to keep this dog. Eventually my dad agreed to let us keep him and we gave him the name Buster. He was like my shadow. It was the most magical experience for me–to have a friend like this. When I went to school, he waited for me to come home. Anywhere I went, Buster went.

It was the best two months of my childhood. Then one weekend, my two cousins came over and I told them how special he was; how he was my dog. My cousins and I decided to walk to the end of the driveway and back, which was a quarter mile each way. At our age, this was a long journey and we wanted to say that we had done it. So we set out to walk to the end of the driveway and back, and of course, Buster decided to tag along with us.

When we reached the end of the driveway, we turned around to head back. Buster had wandered beyond the driveway and into the road. In a flash, a car sped by and hit Buster. All I remember is sliding. The car sliding, trying to stop, and buster sliding from the impact.

I scooped him up and ran all the way home with him. For a young boy, this was a long journey carrying the weight of a dog. He was in such pain. I wish he had been licking me or that in some way we could have been there for each other. But he wasn't. He was resigned and clearly suffering. I was devastated.

My mother and father took him from me and went out onto the back porch. They demanded that I stay inside. I begged my parents to let him live and try to get better but he was so badly injured. His legs were broken, that I knew for sure. But I tried to convince them that the vet could fix it.

From the house, I could hear my mom saying, "He's better now, he's coming around," but my dad said it wouldn't matter. He wasn't going to get better and that Buster would not make it. We couldn't even afford to try anyway.

My father shot him to put him out of his misery. I was absolutely shattered. I was inconsolable for weeks. This was the greatest loss I had ever experienced.

Buster and I were absolutely in tune with each other. It was an instant loyalty, as if we were long time friends that had been reunited.

I've never had the sensation before or since, like the one I had with Buster. He was connected to me and me only.

****

Where do you think he came from?

I've always wondered this. It had to have been a home somewhere nearby, at least within the distance that a dog could travel. We never sorted this part out.

Outside of the material plane, I believe he was my friend from another realm. I knew him.

Why did you name him Buster?

There was no real reason. We just kept trying different names and this one stuck. It just rolled off the tongue. And it worked for him.

CHAPTER 12

Animals and Children

Animals and children have contracts, or agreements, with the Spirit world. At least this has become my conclusion after a decade of holding medium sessions with people trying to connect to the deceased.

We hear about it all the time – someone's loved one passes and the moment they think of them, a butterfly or a cardinal or some other animal or insect appears from nowhere. They are often animals of flight, but not always. People also report their pets almost morphing for a brief moment, taking on the characteristics of a dead human; winking a particular way, or jumping on a chair and putting their arm a certain way, just like the human that passed. Even more stunning is a look, or a glance, we sometimes see in an animal's eyes. Not only do we feel their gaze lock into our soul, but we know that a loved one is there, speaking through their eyes. The expression that the eyes are windows to the soul is true. And because at some point all souls merge into one essence, a lot can be witnessed through this window.

People often wonder if a relative has reincarnated as a particular pet. While my sense is that it is entirely possible for a human to come back as an animal, this is not usually what is going on. Typically the relative is "borrowing" the animal for a brief moment, to make physical contact with us. It is very difficult for spirits to materialize, though it happens. So they need a vessel to "enter" for a moment. That is what I mean when I say that animals have a contract with the spirit world. Animals consent to the favor, they become the vessel, and often carry out visitations for those of us on Earth. Hence the bird or butterfly appearing when we are connected to the thoughts of our loved ones. That thought signals a certain frequency of connection when ourselves, the spirit, and the animal kingdom attune for a moment in time to sync.

Children up to about the age of four or five years old also seem to move about freely between this realm with spirit and the material world.

Tony told me the story of one of his daughter's births. When she arrived, the doctor's handed her to Tony, swaddled and fresh from the womb. He said he held her, and looked deep into her alert eyes. She was his grandmother. Her face with his grandmother's face. At that moment, he looked to his wife and asked if they could give her his grandmother's middle name. His wife agreed. He looked back to his daughter who's eyes smiled back at him. She then took a deep breath and as she exhaled, her face released to take a different form. She was not his grandmother anymore.

One of my favorite stories of another instance of this connection between children and spirit was born of a tragic loss. A client that I was working with had lost a lover to a simple accident. He was walking at the pool, slipped in a puddle, fell back on his head, and died from the injury. It was devastating, as he was at the pool as a favor for his mom. He was visiting a family friend that she thought was important for him to spend time with. He went, but not on his own accord.

The client came to see me as she felt he was trying to make contact with her. At the time of our session, the accident had happened more than three years prior. He did make contact in our session together and they were able to exchange some communication and perhaps work out some closure on the tragedy. But the most beautiful part came a couple years later when she had a baby boy with her new husband.

The client reached out to me to see if I could get a connection on a particular fear her son was having with anything requiring speed – like riding a bike faster than walking or going down a slide. He also wouldn't do anything on wheels without a helmet. Imagine that.

Without drawing any conclusions, I told her that the first and best thing she could do was to just flat out ask her son what he was afraid of and why he didn't want to do these things. She had never thought to do so.

When she next had the opportunity, she asked why he didn't want to go on his bike.

"I fell down and hit my head. Hi Billy. Hi Billy. I fell down and hit my head. Hi Billy. Hi Billy," the son exclaimed.

Billy was the client's name. And she was shocked. Her son had never called her anything other than mommy and he certainly had not fallen down and hit his head.

Billy asked me if I thought her son was her lover reincarnated. I didn't get the sense. I knew his spirit and I knew her son's spirit and they existed independently (though this concept can get a little complex because ultimately we all merge as one in the end). I instead got the sense that her lover was both protecting the child and using the opportunity to communicate with Billy.

We worked together to teach her son that he was safe to try new things but that he could also be careful in doing so. We talked with the deceased lover to acknowledge the protection. Ultimately, the son worked through the fear but seemed to always stay on the cautious side.

I can't say with any kind of authority whether or not the spirit was in fact reincarnated. It's possible that the lover became the son and this kind of information is beyond my sensing abilities. But without a doubt, I can say that spirits work through children often, and that I see this a lot in my work. The story of Billy and her son is just one example of this connection.

When Tony told me the story of Buster, I couldn't help but think about these contracts between spirits and animals. I don't know who or what Buster was, but my senses told me they had met before.

CHAPTER 13

Survival Stars

Once we were deemed safe and efficient with our simulation training, we were advanced to actual flight status. So it was back to the glass balls. They weren't actually glass–they were made of a much thicker, durable substance. They had the same clarity as glass, but we often bumped into things in space and our crafts never broke. I have no idea what technology enabled the craft to "fly". We entered our craft, were pressurized and released into space, worked for the day, then returned and handed off our craft to the service crew. It's shocking how little I knew outside of that process given that I would spend the next nine years of my life either sitting in this glass ball, or confined to my room on the asteroid. When I asked the service crew details about the craft, they said there was a complicated technology, which I vaguely recall as "dual field." But then they would brush me off and tell me there was no point in trying to understand.

I sometimes feel that this part of my experience in outer space gets a little boring to share about. I can't remember as many vivid details as other years in my twenty-year tour, I didn't have any close interpersonal relationships, and I wasn't allowed to stray from the same mundane routine each and every day. To exacerbate this monotony, I was given a handful of minimal video games to fill my time outside of our flight missions. Even more boring than talking about this time, was living through this time. It was mental and physical torture.

The Bureau found a way to simplify what I believe to have been an exceptionally complex and precise process. They gamified our work in the glass balls through the technology of our craft. What we were doing required a scientific precision of exact measurements, a mathematical order, and rigorous dedication to the process that would take hundreds of years and millions, if not billions, of hours of manpower to achieve.

The glass balls that we flew illuminated a radar-type projection of the space and matter around us from an inside "screen". When we got close to where we were working, everything around us was turned off on this screen aside from what we were intended to work with on that particular flight mission. Certain rocks would glow and the gravity well target was alway highlighted purple.

We got scored on our work each day. Both precision and volume factored into the score. There was a little bit of an art to achieving a high score. You had to both select the best rocks, but also push the right number of rocks. If you obsessed with finding the exact right element and did not move enough volume, this would deduct from your total.

The first flight out, we only worked for about an hour. We were instructed to propulse three objects each into the gravity well, then we flew back in formation together. We could talk to each other while working and to pass the time. We made our own kind of games as well, as if we were in competition with each other. Simple things, like challenging each other to stay in formation while upside down, or sideways, or who could fly the closest. We could communicate with each other as we worked and there was an element of teasing and talking shit that also entertained us. Later on, we would compete with each other for who could move the most material.

This first short trip out is where we actually learned that we were not the only crew. There was a non-stop rotation of others like us–so the project was a perpetual effort.

The next day we went out and did a full shift. It was the equivalent of seven or eight hours of pushing space rocks towards the gravity well. This shift is where we realized that we weren't very good at our mission. It was much more difficult than the simulation training and the space rocks looked very different than they did in the simulators. They were much more irregularly shaped. Many times, as soon as we touched the rocks with the craft arms, they would break into thousands of pieces. It began to feel like a hopeless job.

Sometimes for months at a time we were instructed to push certain elements. We could pull detailed reports of the space rocks to see which were good to push and which met the requirements for the daily mission as far as their elemental components.

We knew we were building a star, but sometime in this roughly eight year period, we learned that we were pushing mass into this gravity field so that it would eventually ignite. Hence the order of our work and the science to it.

Ships would come in from other places in space to bring in elements that were needed but not available in our working scope as well. They would dump them in the sky and we would push them towards the well, just like the rocks. I never actually saw any of the ships, but they appeared like a cereal box in the graphic on my glass ball screen. There were times that they were nearby when we approached, but they always took off before we got there. I wouldn't have been able to see them anyhow, unless they were emitting a lot of light.

We realized other ships were helping because we'd "work" an area and clear all the rocks, then return later and it will be full again. When we asked Command about this, they admitted we were getting help from other parts of space. These materials were coming from within the same nebula or at least from a nearby nebula.

Layer by layer, element by element, gas by gas, the Bureau was attempting to build their survival star.

It wasn't just about building a star. We needed to construct it so that it was small and the power output in the star's early stage of life would be stable. In order for the Bureau to continue life in this region of space, they needed to be able to construct bases around this artificial star without intense solar flares and ejections from the star. They had built one before, but it took a million years for the star to stabilize, so they were not able to develop their civilization in close proximity to it. The star had violent storms and would have disrupted any chance of orbital life nearby.

The next stage of the project would be to build a ring around this star so that objects could be placed in orbit around it after the star stabilized.

The Bureau was in an irregular galaxy behind the M51 that was not spiral shaped, but instead a ball. Because of this, stars were not forming. There was a lot of space material that in other galaxies, would have become stars. But the stars that did form in the ball galaxy decayed faster and they knew that sooner or later, the galaxy would become all material and no stars. They needed them for light and for life.

There was a regular spiral galaxy right next door, but we were told that we were not welcome there. It was a galaxy at war and The Bureau were a peaceful species. So it was a matter of survival to manufacture stars in our galaxy that we owned outright. This was our claimed region of space. We needed to make it work here.

So this star manufacturing process had been going on for a long time, and I believe all recruits like me were brought on to finish the project on time. It went on for essentially eight or nine years. We flew eight hour shifts, came back, went to our rooms in isolation, ate, showered sometimes, played video games, then went to bed. We were woken up by the lights coming on and under our beds, where we would find our fresh, clean uniform for the next day.

Over time, my crew did get better with selecting and pushing the space rocks, as well as perfecting the selection of solid rocks that wouldn't break when we made contact. This was something we got a feel for, and not because it was scientific or taught to us. But we could lock in on objects with our screens then examine the color patterns as they illuminated on the radar. We could start to sense which would likely hold shape when we pushed. This process alone tells me that as this being, I had a sense of intuition, of higher mental processing–though I can't say I felt connected to it during that time. This intuition was beyond my level of awareness, but I relied on it without realizing it.

CHAPTER 14

The Raft in Harrison

In 1979, when I was 7 years old, my parents decided to take the family camping in Harrison, Michigan. My mom was busy setting up our tent and my mom was preparing to make dinner on the grill. We had only been there a few hours and my sister had already made friends with a girl a few campsites down named Candy. She and Candy wanted to take a small raft out on the lake, and I pleaded with my sister to let me go with them. I didn't have any friends yet and I had nothing to do, plus it was my older sister and I often wanted to tag along.

My mom overheard us arguing and intervened, telling my sister, June, that if she wanted to go with Candy, she had to take me along. So it was settled and June, Candy, and I headed for the lake with our inflatable raft.

We started to paddle out into the lake when some neighboring, older boys decided to mess with us. They first threw a dead, decomposing fish into our raft. Instead of engaging with them, Candy, June, and I decided to paddle out further in the lake to get away from them.

We weren't paying close attention and one of the boys swam up from under the raft and knocked us over. We were pretty far into the lake at this point and I didn't know how to swim. Candy was able to quickly flip the raft back over and pull herself inside, but in doing so, Candy had pushed herself and the raft further away from us.

It happened very quickly, and at first, I was flailing around keeping myself near enough to the surface to get breaths–but I was struggling to stay afloat. I was sinking. June was near me and I grabbed her hair at one point to lift myself up for a breath of air, but then I immediately started to go under. She was fighting me off to keep herself above water and as soon as she got free from my grip, she swam away from me. I was all alone. I was trying to figure out how to swim, but it was useless.

I remember sinking down pretty far. I looked up as I went down and could see the distorted rays of the sun glistening through the water. But the light was getting smaller and smaller. Nothing was working. And then I gave up. I closed my eyes and sank.

Then I saw somebody from above me. A girl reached her hand down into the water and told me to start kicking, not to give up now. I had somewhere to be. And I needed to cut the shit. I could swim. I just needed to kick.

She had long brown hair that reached down to me in the water. It was floating about me so beautifully. And I knew she was my friend. So I started kicking.

I got close enough to the surface to grab my sister again and pull myself up to get a breath. There must have been a lot of commotion at the surface as my dad was now in the lake. He took hold of me and swam me to shore. All the other parents from the camping sights around the lake had come out to see what was going on.

June walked over to me and I asked her anxiously, "Where's Jackie?"

She looked not just confused but repulsed, "Who's Jackie? What are you even talking about? My friend is Candy."

"She helped me. In the water, she was the one who helped me."

I could see that what I was saying was both confusing and slightly annoying everyone around me and they all hushed me, guiding me back towards our site.

"There's no Jackie here."

CHAPTER 15

The Catwalk

In 1979, I was not even born. But I was at the raft because time is not linear and souls are not bound to a single lifetime. And I remember this incident, almost the way Tony tells it.

I want to first start by saying that both Tony and I do not feel that we have played overly significant roles in each other's stories-in this life or any lives before or future. There may be places where it would feel to the reader that we are alluding to the notion that we are some kind of bound souls. But neither of us do.

We do, however, feel that it's possible we have crossed each other's paths many times before. And while not directly relevant to this particular book, I saw Tony in a past life regression I did with Mira Kelly, roughly six months before we became friends. In this past life, I was a writer in France Post-World War II and liked to drink espresso and smoke cigarettes. Tony was my writing teacher for a short time and taught me to write the truth–not to attempt to elicit any particular emotion–but to just tell the story matter of fact.

In my regression, Mira asked me if I knew my writing teacher from other lives and I told her yes, but that I didn't recognize him. She asked me if there was something I could identify to help me remember who this person was, and I said yes, his beard.

Then a few months later, Tony and I became friends. It was around March of 2019 when I reached out to him after watching an episode of Cosmic Disclosure on Gaia TV, which is like the Netflix of spirituality.

Our friendship developed slowly, over time. I would go months without getting in touch, then we'd connect over a phone call or text when I'd come to him with deep or compelling information I had uncovered. I was heavily researching the phenomenon of the twenty-year tour to make sense of some of my own unusual abilities, "dreams", and experiences. So we became close and eventually we started joking that we should have been neighbors so we could pop in for coffee and a chat.

Not long after, we started to record our conversations

and post them on YouTube for others who might be interested in our topics and research. Then YouTube started censoring information so we moved to Patreon. Not long after starting our Patreon, I agreed to help Tony with completing his book. He'd been slowly compiling his story for six years but it was nowhere near "book ready."

It wasn't until I finally met Tony in person for a conference in Mt. Shasta that I recognized the beard. He picked me up from the airport to drive out to the conference location and I distinctly remember the moment I caught the side profile of his beard and it hit me—I remembered—he's my teacher from France.

And it dawned on me that I had told Tony more times than I could count while working on the book that he needed to, "Just tell the truth and not worry about what anyone thinks. Just tell the truth."

While I was both shocked and excited to have put it all together, Tony quickly brushed me off, mostly I think because that's what friends do. I often joke with Tony that he doesn't take me and my experiences seriously. But I think when you go through so much, not much impresses you. You've seen it all. And a part of you believes it all, because you know what's possible. So there's no shock factor in anything anyone tells you.

The raft incident is mind blowing to me still. In Eastern

religions and teachings, there are many documented instances of bi-location and time play. Many Gurus are well known for this kind of "trickery" and thousands of people have experienced something similar to what Tony and I experienced with the raft.

I think it's also important to call out the differences in the way both Tony and I experienced the incident. I think memory is bound by the restrictions of all other life experiences we've had. An example of this would be an architect visiting a botanical garden and noticing the curvature of the atrium. While a botanist visiting the same garden might notice the rare species of plants they were growing. Both people went to the same place, but both had different experiences and therefore would remember the visit differently. But it doesn't make the botanical garden different. The fact that Tony and I recall the same event differently makes more sense than if we had both remembered it exactly the same. And I feel the same can be said for things like abductions and twenty-year tours. Just because two or multiple people recall the experience differently does not mean the event is not occurring.

Plus when you communicate through telepathy, which we typically do in altered states (and so do spirits in medium sessions), it's more like a transfer of thought information. Not words. We have to then translate this form of communication into words, which has a way of breaking things apart.

There's an important document floating around the internet called the "The Analysis and Assessment of the Gateway Process." Within this document, information is presented about human consciousness expansion and the mechanics of this process. The Gateway experience was created by Bob Monroe, who founded the Monroe Institute. Tony shared the document with me (that you can usually find through a quick Google search) and after reading, we agreed to try a Gateway recording at the same time on the same night to see if we could meet on the moon. Our goal was to see if a part of my consciousness had been split and was currently existing in outer space, which is the basic principle of the twenty-year tour that Tony endured.

So we set our time to begin the Gateway recording, which was still accessible on YouTube at that time. I was in Dallas, Texas, and Tony was in Michigan. Our plan was to start the recording at the same time, enter an expanded state of consciousness, then astral travel and meet each other on the moon.

It took me some time, but I was able to "get" to the moon. What surprised me, confused me actually, was that there was a catwalk when I got there. And Tony was standing on the catwalk. I was delighted to see him. It worked, it actually fucking worked.

Tony and I wanted to see if we teamed up, if we could either remote view or actually find another aspect of me in space. I approached Tony on the catwalk. I was hovering, flying maybe even. And I went to reach for his hand to travel together, but he was stuck. He was dense and immoveable. I focused in on him in a way that felt like merging consciousness for a brief moment and immediately found myself beneath a raft, watching Tony as a young child struggling to get air. He was flailing about, taking a breath, then going under, fighting for survival.

I grabbed his arm, "Tony, hey, calm down. Calm down. You have to relax. We need to go and we can't if you're panicking."

I wasn't speaking verbally, there was too much water. We were talking though our minds.

He kept freaking out, so I grabbed him underwater.

"Tony! We have things to do. Snap out of it. This isn't it."

Then I found myself on the catwalk, staring Tony's adult self in the eyes. He was almost catatonic. I tried to pick him up and take him with me but I couldn't. It was like the catwalk was pulling him down. For whatever reason, I felt like I had a decision to make. I could stay there with him, or I could continue my journey in my altered state. I wanted to travel. But I couldn't leave Tony like that.

So I made a compromise. I reached my hand out to adult Tony, frozen on the catwalk. And then I did something. Something that state of myself knew how to do, but that Jackie on Earth can't recognize or explain. I broke the pull from under Tony, and he became weightless again. He wasn't stuck to the catwalk, but he also wasn't ready to come with me.

I did continue on my journey that night, leaving Tony behind. I did not find an altered state of myself on that trip.

When Tony and I spoke on the phone the next day, we reported back to each other what we experienced.

"Did you ever almost drown, Tony?"

"No."

"Never? In a raft?"

"Wait, yes, kind of. I did. It was…weird…wait…" his voice slowed.

"Holy fuck. You're Jackie."

CHAPTER 16

The Lies

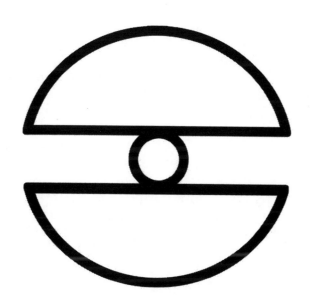

By about month six of full-time flight work, I was granted access to the entire menu of the computer. There were full immersion multiplayer games and some of the other players were on other asteroids or planets throughout our region of space. I knew this because we could interact with people in the game, but the vocabulary was still limited and restricted to preset options like: leave me alone, hi how are you, etc.

After about a year, a new version of one of the games came out where we were able to share three or four words of our choosing. It was a very basic game. The whole purpose of the game was to go out and collect things that gave you some kind of advantage. For example, you could find a token that made you taller. Or you could change your appearance, your walking speed, or little things like that. And even though mundane, these games were important because they are how we all eventually realized that we were in deep shit.

Everything felt hunky dory for a few years. Especially as the games got better. Eventually hundreds of us doing the same flight missions found each other in the game and even though we couldn't talk much, we were beginning to put things together over time.

Then the vibe started to shift. Our Commanders

began to reprimand us, insisting that our production was falling behind. And I shared this troubled news once in the game.

"I'm sad. We're behind," I stated.

Then someone said, "everyone is behind everywhere."

The briefings that we were receiving from our superiors, however, said that our squadron was the only one that was behind and that all the others were on schedule. They were riding us about it for weeks, how behind we were.

I shared this again one day in the game and another player replied that that's what they tell everyone. In disbelief, I told my colleagues in the fleet the next day that I was beginning to think that they were lying to us. At first they didn't believe me, but then they did what I did and asked through the game. They all got told the same thing. Our commanders were gaslighting us. And they were lying to us. It wasn't true that our squadron was the only one behind–or at least we weren't the only squadron being told that.

When the Commanders found out, I got in pretty serious trouble for telling my colleagues. Part of my punishment was that I was restricted from multi-player games. In fact, we all were.

This punishment lasted for the next few months. Eventually we got the game back, but we were no longer able to talk to others through the system. Other people could interact, but not us. And that was the end of the games being a happy part of my life.

Around year seven, our superiors started briefing us on ways to get more things done. They were also modifying the ships to try to enable us to get more work done faster. The project actually was desperately behind, but it always had been. Up until this point, they had been punishing us to get us to go faster. But now, they started working with us to help us go faster.

We were instructed to now start cabling rocks together to propulse conglomerates into the gravity well–to get more mass into the field faster. This was a technique we actually learned by accident, that we could spin rocks together towards the target.

The ships had a lot of cable on them that we would sometimes tie around the space rocks. We would pull them behind us for some time then detach the cable and let the rocks continue on the trajectory towards the gravity well.

One time, one of our flight crew had tied one large rock to another in an attempt to push them both at the same time. But he released them at an angle, and the cluster actually began to spin. It collected other rocks as it spiraled toward the target so that by the time it hit, it was much larger than when we initially released it. The gravity well was also ten times larger than it was when I started the project, so it was easier to hit the target.

So this became our method. We created a sort of bolo with cables and a larger rock tied around a small cluster of rocks. We would then catapult this object towards the well.

In doing so, we were able to get the project caught up. Which is amazing to ponder–we learned by accident hundreds of years into a project that there was a much more efficient way to hurl mass. It was also the single factor that pushed the project to success. Had we not discovered the bolo method, the project would have terminated. More accurately, we would have failed to create a star, or created an extremely unstable, unusable star.

At some point during my time there, I was told by other pilots through the multi-player game that I was taken from somewhere else. They told me that I would go back to a home planet and return to a life in a biome, or an atmospheric planet. We didn't think much of it, because we were told that we had chosen this mission, and that everyone in the project had done the same. It also had a bit of an urban legend feeling about it. Because of that, we didn't know what to believe so we didn't latch on to the idea too much while we were there.

When we finally got caught up and were about six months from ignition–meaning enough mass was hurled in the right order for a star to ignite–we started talking amongst ourselves, asking each other what we each thought would happen next.

We noticed simultaneously that friends in the game that we knew were working on the same project had started coming up missing. When we asked our superiors in person about them, they avoided the question altogether. But we pressed them and eventually we were told that our friends were reassigned. We found this confusing because their ten years were up and we believed they were supposed to go home.

As we got closer and closer to the star ignition, our superiors began presenting options for next assignments to those of us who kept the highest scores. It was then that we learned that there was no going home. That this technology could be used on repeat in ten year increments, indefinitely. We could be there for fifty to sixty years, at minimum. I was eighth in ranking on scores so my options were limited on my reassignment.

We also learned that many other corporations were involved with building the star. It was not just the Bureau building the star. We had actually been contracted to this project. It was another lie.

And these new reassignments were all over the place, doing completely different things. We could be contracted to run a digger, excavating a planet, every day, for another ten years. The assignments felt boring. Which is almost unimaginable after spending ten years in the monotony of this project. It was utter dread.

I went berserk. I would go to my room and lose my shit, then I would get the light. If we complained, we would get the light. The light was everywhere. And it was unbearable. In less than two minutes in the light, you'd be on the floor crying. We were about a month out from ignition and I got the light pretty often during that last month. Some guys stayed under the light too long and they were severely injured. It caused a form of a burn where big chunks of their skin would flake off. They were the equivalent of hospitalized after that, and required rehab to heal. Some guys thought they could mentally outlast the light, but the longer it went, the more damaging it became. The more stubborn you were, the more injury you sustained.

They often told us that there was no way to end it. Suicide was impossible and not even worth trying. There were even guys that got the light in their ship because they were essentially trying to crash it. They were then taken upon return and punished all night. A couple guys never came back. My sense is that they were automatically reassigned, not killed. The Bureau could now afford to lose men, because we were now ahead of schedule.

****

Do you know if you would have remained in that alien body if you went to a second ten year service term? As that life form?

That was my understanding, yes. But what I learned

113

was that I couldn't trust anything they said to me. I assume I would have simply been reassigned with the same body and the same consciousness.

Do you get the sense that other life forms live a different duration of life than humans?

Absolutely. I think we live relatively short lives compared to what I learned about out there. In fact, there were often comments about how short our lifetimes are on Earth. I believe this was probably intentional. When you consider the perspective of a soul incarnating, it's desirable to have a short life in my opinion. You don't have to get as much right, not like you would if you were choosing a life and a life form for one-thousand years. It's like a nice test drive.

What do you think about references in the Bible of people who lived to be hundreds of years old?

Yes, exactly. Noah lived to be more than 500 years old—950 years old I think. Or so says the book of Genesis. I think that they were the original hybrid species and that they did actually live to be that age. And that we've been somehow downgraded. Personally, I don't know how or why this process happens. But I think it's entirely possible, and even likely that it does. It's also entirely possible that someone could still live to be that old and they could easily hide it, and we'd never know. You'd just need someone to grant you a new identity, which isn't hard to do if you were connected to a person of authority.

The sad truth is that our lives are being shortened currently. The age of life expectancy actually went down. In 2018, it was 78 years. In 2022 it was 77 years in the US, UK, and Canada.

CHAPTER 17

Ignition

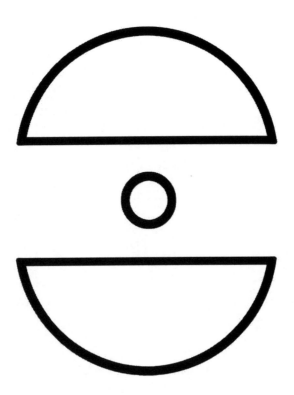

We knew that star ignition was near. We were briefed about it daily and understood that we were less than a few weeks out.

On the day of ignition, the activity of the operation was at an all time high. Other fleets of ships were there streaming in additional resources, material, and gas. On an average day of the project, only five to ten percent of available ships would be visiting and dropping off materials. But today, they were all here.

When a star ignites, it sucks in everything around it within a certain radius. We worked fifteen percent inside of this blast radius and were pushing material into the target right up to the very last moment. The gravity well was building at an exponential rate now and even the gas from our nebula began to get sucked in. Because of this, we could start to see stars in the distance, which had formerly been blocked by the opaque gaseous substance around us. It was nice to have reference points for once, as I was used to blackness. I hoped that when I finally saw a star, that it would be beautiful. But it wasn't. It was actually completely underwhelming.

We asked if there was a safety feature that would automatically retract our glass ball ships when ignition was certain. We were told no, that there would be a timer with a "minimum safe time" to manually retract on our screen. We were to return to base before the timer ended. Our base was also actively traveling away from the gravity field to stay at a safe distance. The time needed to get away from the pull of ignition and safely back to base would all be displayed for us.

It became evident to me that this was an opportunity to kill myself. And I spent the last few days of the mission building up the courage to do exactly this. Even up until the last minute, I wasn't sure if I would or could do it. I had no idea what killing myself meant for me, or my soul, which I was acutely aware of. We had been shown simulations of the ignition and I knew without a shadow of a doubt that if I stayed within the working field, I would ignite as well.

What I knew for certain was that we were being lied to. And that my superiors who were lying to me were also lying to their superiors. I didn't know why. But I could trust no one.

Our games stopped altogether in the final week. Because the Bureau stopped caring about us. It was like we were dead men walking. They quit talking to us altogether. Whereas before, someone high in Command would pop into the training every few days to check in on us, now meetings ceased altogether. I began to seriously fear what would come next. The past ten years had been unbearable. I couldn't face ten more, let alone an indefinite number more. I kept thinking about the other guys' attempts to kill themselves. I started to realize that I might not have as clear of an opportunity to end my life in upcoming assignments. If I did it now, in this way, I would be vaporized–instantly and without pain.

On the final day, I was slinging rocks into the gravity field when they began calling us back. But instead of going back, I went deeper into the well. I called in that I was going to help other guys. They told me I was going to be in trouble when I got back. I told them that my craft was having problems and I could not go back. There was nothing I could do–I couldn't help it.

Command ran a remote diagnostic and reported that nothing was wrong. But I stayed where I was while everyone else was going back. My crew was already half way back to base when both Command and my crew realized what was going on. There wasn't enough time to send someone back to get me. There was a point when they just stopped bothering me.

And it became peaceful.

Then the fear of dying hit me. But I also knew that even if I turned back then, I was too far into the blast zone to come out. I started traveling slowly further into the field. I got sad again, accepting that there was no turning back now, even if I changed my mind. I realized that I was about to die. I started to question if my next assignment would have been happier, then reassuring myself that this was the right thing to do. And the timer continued to count down. The same timer I saw while I was drugged on the plane in Peru. The same timer I would see on Earth when I got sick as a child.

And then I saw a blast of white light.

CHAPTER18

Her

It felt like my body got washed away from me but who I was stood still. In the same spot. I was fully conscious, but had no memory of anything before that moment. I felt like I was standing inside a room bathed in light. It was bright. Not the darkness that I experienced in Peru.

I could form though, but had no context of what I was. I knew I was real, but could remember nothing. I was formless, but I had full consciousness.

I heard a child's voice ask, "Who am I? What is this?" from somewhere else.

It felt like it was behind me. But there was also no

direction where I was.

Then the voice came closer and aske, "Who are you?"

I answered, "I don't know."

"What are you?"

"I don't know."

"What do you want?"

I felt much smaller than this thing. But it had a child's voice. Then it left me for a second and traveled around before asking me again, "Who are all they?"

It could see things that I couldn't.

Then it came back to me, angry now, and said "What do you want here?"

I told her, "I just want to be your friend."

"What is a friend?"

"I don't know for sure but I don't mean you any harm."

It was upset because it couldn't leave our place. It was trapped in our vicinity. It saw other beings but couldn't go and communicate with them.

I tried to comfort it, "At least you have me here. You're not alone. And you are okay."

It seemed to have access to more information than I had.

Then other voices came. They were very loud, and older.

"What has happened here?" they demanded.

The older voices were furious. They kept pressing to know what had been done and how this had happened.

"What have you done?" they kept asking. It felt directed at me, but also at everything. There was a sense of desperation.

They were shouting amongst themselves and then I clearly heard a female voice say, "The dwellers built it."

Then the child's voice defended, "Nobody built me, I'm me. I'm just like you."

A loud male voice spoke over the child's voice and said, "You be quiet."

Then he approached me, forcefully, and asked who I was.

"I'm her friend," I said.

He told me that she was a complete abomination. She wouldn't live more than the blink of an eye. The older voices were both angry and devastated.

Then it was as if he grabbed me and threw me into the dead of space, away from them all. The light disappeared.

I was in complete darkness and silence. I couldn't see or feel anything. I was in a state of limbo. Completely out of body. But somehow I knew this place. I'd been here before. It felt like hours went by, maybe centuries. Time doesn't make sense in this realm. I was totally by myself–absolute aloneness. I didn't know what, but I had the sense that I was waiting and that something was going to come next.

Then the child's voice came to me and told me that they had taught her how to move. She came to see me to tell me this while they were deciding what to do with her. She told me they might kill her–she didn't know.

All I wanted to do was to make sure that we were still friends and that I hadn't gotten her in trouble.

"Yes, we're friends. We'll always be friends. I have to go back so they can teach me more and decide what they want to do with me. If I can come back again, I will. And I'll find you."

I keep calling it "her", but she was really more androgynous. They all were actually. But if there was a spectrum of male to female, they seemed to fall more to one side than the other on the spectrum.

I was confused. I couldn't grasp onto any reasoning. While I can recall it all now, at the time, information would come and then it would go and I couldn't keep linear time and coalesce the experience or information. The passage of time was also bewildering. Again, the whole experience could have been years. Or it could have been minutes. It felt like a long time. It was like a rolodex of experiences both constantly spinning but also stopping for flashes of a moment that I could experience at the same time. I kept forgetting what I was. And had nothing to contrast these happenings against–meaning there was nothing to reference my setting. No memory of anything different.

The child's voice came back again just before I returned to my body, but this time it was older. It told me that it had lived hundreds of thousands of years now and that they had finally decided what they were going to do about it.

They said that because I worked on the project, and she was not a natural phenomenon, that she was destined for a short life. The place where the voices exist is one of profound love with each other. They were all deeply connected. Because she was going to live a short life and they knew it, it was going to cause the voices a great deal of pain. Both the fact that she wouldn't live long and that they had to exist knowing this information was going to hurt them.

As punishment, every single one of us that worked on the project to create the artificial star was going to experience the same pain of her death in at least one of our lives. She told me that it would be her in particular for me, and asked if she could be in one of my lives. I felt an instant connection and loyalty to her and told her that she could be in all of them.

She asked if I meant it.

And I said, "Yes, you're my friend."

"Even if it's short, and you're hurt by all of my deaths?"

And I said it was okay because that meant I would see her in the next life.

She left, telling me that she was going to ask.

She was gone for even longer this time. It felt like ten thousand years. I did nothing during that time. Just existed as a consciousness, floating through space. When she came back, she told me she had good and bad news.

She could be in each of my lives as long as her original form existed. She knew that my original form lived longer. But she would always die before me in my incarnations.

Her consciousness had not been diluted into lifetimes yet, but mine was. I was headed back to a lifetime that I had come from. And in this lifetime I was returning to, she had permission to go there and meet me. In fact, she had special permission in this lifetime to do whatever she wanted–and she was going to help me.

"I'll see you there. Goodbye."

Then she left. It felt like another hundred thousand years passed by. There's no way to describe the passage of time. Or the loneliness.

At some point, I returned to my body, right in the same room on Ceres. I woke up on the slanted table where I'd received the two needles. They pulled the needles out and walked me right back to the barracks. I was told I had the rest of the weekend off and to rest. I remembered nothing of it at the time. I simply walked through the door, back into the hallway. It was back to work as usual for me after that.

The only thing I knew of the trade project from that point forward was that the deal was cancelled because of multiple suicides on the other end. But Ceres Colony considered it a success because they had enough personnel to honor their agreement and get paid out something like 70% of the agreement.

****

At what point did you remember the Project Starmaker life?

I need to first start by saying that my memories in this timeline aren't as clear as my memories in the Ceres timeline. I have way less detail recall. For example, I know my species had a name, but I can't remember it. And we had names, they were stupid, but I don't remember mine.

When I was a kid on earth, I got sick every Easter. Good Friday to be exact. And when I got sick, I would hallucinate. I would see the timer during my hallucinations. I didn't make anything of it, but it did disturb me. It was an intense memory that didn't make any sense to me. I just got up and watched Bugs Bunny and forgot about it.

The full story came through when I was 43, in what I would call a cluster recall phase. A lot of memories had come through after an MRI scan of just my head and when I thought about the timer during that phase of my Earth based life, the rest of the memories around it came through.

Why do you think it's so maddening to remember the life? As in, why were the men coming out into the hallway so disturbed?

I suspect the most disturbed guys must have stayed longer than ten years. Maybe fifty years or longer in hard labor. And most of them probably had to commit suicide to come back. Or endure a lifetime of suffering. Not all guys who came back were hysterical. I think remembering a suicide is traumatic.

Do you think it's a good or a bad thing that we don't remember all of our lives?

I think it's a good thing. A blessing actually. But like everything, also a curse. The knowledge you would have would be a blessing. And I think it's a blessing to not carry over bad habits from past lives.

But the regrets you'd have would be a curse. You'd have so much baggage.

There was a time in history when ritualistic human sacrifice was very normal and acceptable. If certain groups of people were reincarnating with their past life memories intact, they may find something as barbaric as this to be completely normal and acceptable. Remembering all phases of our history as a species would normalize a lot of really unacceptable things in modern times.

The people that I witnessed in Seattle were very established in all of their endeavors. It was as if they'd had time to live multiple lives in just this one on earth. They were ahead of everyone else in a way.

What did the loud voice mean that she wouldn't live very long?

This was because their layering strategy had failed even though the star would be extremely stable in its early life, it would eventually nova very young. The lifespan of our sun is 10 billion years and this star we built was smaller, so I can't estimate what "short" means but I would imagine it's still in the millions of years.

What do you make of the space being light when you first meet the voices, especially because when you first entered a similar space on the flights in Peru, it was a dark room?

Well, worth noting, is that I entered the dark room from the flights on Peru from a place of light. I'm not sure what this means, but I was different from the things in the room. And at some stage of visiting this dark room over the course of the two years that I took the flights, a voice of authority entered and commanded the desperate energies to leave me alone. The voice gave me some kind of authority that I eventually learned to command every time I entered the room. In fact, at some point, I looked forward to the IV because I became both lucid and in control when I went to the other side. Looking forward to it is actually not quite accurate because I started getting sicker and sicker after the flights. At first, I didn't feel well for a day or two after the IVs. But towards the end, I would sometimes stay sick the entire month until the next flight.

Also, towards the end of the two years, without fail, before I left the dark room to re-enter my body, I always saw the timer countdown.

I think the way they were forcing me into this place was a crime. Both a crime against humanity to force a child to do such things, but also a crime against who we are as spiritual consciousness entities. I think each of us has a natural process to get to this place, which can be achieved in various ways: plant medicine, deep meditation, near death experiences. But it's still a process and there is still an element of natural flow and even possibly the soul's consent to enter.

I think because I was being unnaturally forced into this place so frequently, some kind of energy authority entered and made it right. I think that there are regulators of many immaterial things like time travel, consciousness connection, traversing multiple realms, etc. And in my case, something intervened in that dark room I went to on the flights and helped me–helped my spirit–with the unfairness.

When you were taken near death at Inyokern, was this the place you visited?

It was the exact same place. But I can't remember it. But I know.

CHAPTER 19

Our Original Source

The story that follows is, in my humble opinion, the reason this book came to be. And the book before this one, *Ceres Colony Cavalier.*

Tony and I realized at some point in our friendship that he and I were visited by non-Earth based beings in the same week, maybe even the same day, prior to knowing each other. And these visitations were critical to both of our journeys in that we were both told to move forward with sharing our respective truths– Tony's truth of having been abducted, and my truth of possessing extrasensory abilities to communicate with dead people.

Tony was visited by an extraterrestrial in his bedroom

in Hawaii and I walked out of my New York City office to sit on a pier of the Husdon River, where I found myself talking to five ethereal entities. I was bargaining with them. This was in September of 2017, and Tony and I were not yet acquaintances.

While on the pier, I felt an instruction from them to use my gifts for good but I was pleading with them to promise me that I would never harm anyone through this connection and to please make my financial future viable if I were to embrace this path. At the time, I had a promising, high paying NYC career.

I had only led a handful of medium sessions at that point, and mostly for practice, but the clarity of what came through was disturbing. I was unsettled by the reality of my connection to the unseen and the accuracy of the information I was receiving from the deceased. I understand that a lot of people wish to have psychic abilities, but the truth is, they can be unnerving. Because you become no longer like the rest. And the reality you've relied on no longer provides safety. There is no "truth" anymore and everything you've ever assumed falls under intense scrutiny.

The five entities assured me that a path would be made. People would be hurt, because this is unavoidable. My experience in Peru hurt badly. But it was necessary for me and it changed my life for the better. What they did promise me was that when I worked with them, we would always operate from a place of love and the highest truth.

So I walked back to my office and turned in my resignation. And for the most part, the five entities have guided my path ever since.

When I shared this experience on the piers with Tony a few years later, we agreed that maybe I could work to figure out what the five entities were, and that trying hypnotic regression for this purpose could be helpful.

The following transcription is from a hypnotic regression I underwent early 2021. It picks up mid-regression after being prompted to define who or what the five are. As we pick up, I am talking to one of the five.

Hypnotist (H): Were you one of these beings in a past life?

Jackie (J): My soul is still there. But my awareness is here.

H: Why did Jackie decide to come to earth? Why did you want to do it?

J: He said a lot of things very quickly. He said you always liked adventure. You believed you can help. I can help. What else?

H: How about, was there a certain mission you had to do?

J: Yes, he said I already kind of understand it. Yeah, we have different skills there. That are the norm. And I brought some here because they're really powerful in vibrational work. Like when we meet there, we share all present moments* that we've had, and that's a skill that I remembered here.

*What I meant by we "share all present moments that we've had" is that as an alternative life form, when we first greeted each other, we would share every life experience we'd already had as well as the feelings it gave us and the impact it had on us through a sort of telepathic transfer. I called these experiences "all present moments" because in that life form, we understood that time is not linear and that we are always experiencing the present.

H: Ask if your other aspect of yourself is located there with him. In that base or facility?

J: NO! No. Out of the galaxy.

H: Ok, don't go traveling just yet.

J: It's very far. I can see it. It's very far. If you imagined our whole galaxy the size of a dime, this place is a hundred feet away. Very far.

H: Is it a universe or a galaxy?

J: It's a space we don't understand. It's an energy space we don't understand.

H: Is it another dimension, maybe?

J: It's a way we don't really comprehend energy. We would just see it as darkness. But it's not.

H: Obviously you were meant to go, so let's continue traveling. You may want to accelerate, otherwise we could be here for a while. Keep increasing your speed to get there.

J: No. You go there in an instant. I am here. It is not a long trip. I have met my guides here before. It's the dark, hovering space. I just did not know.

H: Ok, go ahead and approach your aspect of yourself. Can you tell me, is it a ship?

J: No! It's just space.

H: Ok, how is your other self occupying this space?

J: I'm a silvery-blue light. I'm actually enjoying it. Which is kind of a relief.

H: Alright, so do you see your other self?

J: No, just light. It's like a light. Like an amoeba. Big, though. But I can talk to myself.

H: Ok, so go ahead and introduce yourself as Jackie from the year 2021 and planet Earth. State that you're here to learn if there are any messages for yourself. Or to ask questions to yourself. What would be the first question you would have?

J: A lot happens very quickly. A conversation has already been had.

Long pause.

She's enjoying this. It's not a she but I have to use she to explain her. She's enjoying this and that makes me feel relieved. She's saying not to worry. And asking me why I don't embrace the Earth reality more. I told her that I don't want to be ridiculed. She told me that this causes myself so much heartache. I told her this is all hard for me to believe. She told me this is part of what I signed up for. "But what's the point?" I asked her. And then it stopped.

H: What other questions would you have for that aspect for yourself?

J: Why does this all make me feel crazy? How do I know that I'm not hallucinating?

Long pause.

And all she's saying is to remember this color. And then getting bigger*. And showing me the color.

*When she became bigger, she became the size of a sun–or larger, even.

H: And what's the color?

J: It's this silvery blue with maybe a little green.

H: Is that the trigger to get access on your own? To connect to your community of origin?

J: She said I only need to connect to me. But I want my guides. And she said it's not really how it works when you go this far. But I want them. I feel alone without my guides.

H: But you're not really alone.

J: I know that. But there have always been four others before. But now I went further. To just my source energy.

H: Now that you've shared your consciousness, are

there any other messages that your other aspect of yourself would like you to know?

J: Ok.

Long pause.

She said that Earth is in trouble. And I know that. I can feel that. It causes a lot of fear for me. But she said it's been in trouble from its inception. There has never been pure or natural...energy here.* She told me this "trouble" is not new, so I need no fear so much. It's not new. And she's just telling me to remember my sense of adventure. Sometimes when things feel scary, to instead see them as an adventure.

*She (or I) was showing me that the earth was not in a natural state. We, humans, are not a natural phenomenon. The earth was made by intelligent species. Humans were crafted to inhabit this Earth. And while the Earth as a planet did form naturally, that it had long since been altered to support specific intentions and specific life. And the intentions behind which these alterations were made were the main source of the "trouble."

H: Ok, so to connect to origin. Ask her the fastest way to connect to origin if there was one.

J: Well, this is not the same as connecting to the five.

This is connection to my source energy.

[end transcript]

It took me a few days to integrate this regression before I called Tony to discuss.

"I'm not sure anymore that I'm a starseed, Tony," I admitted.

I had been considering the notion that I was an alien species before and that I made a journey to Earth, to live as a human, for reasons defined by my soul. I think this makes a lot of sense given that energy is never really created or terminated, but instead just changes form. At least through the science that we understand. It seems possible that who we are as energy bodies has existed since the beginning of time, but that it changes form, or bodies, as it traverses the galaxies.

"I think who I really am is actually a star. I saw myself as that. I was a miniscule and also immeasurably gigantic ball of light in the darkness. I was so fluid. So certain."

And what came next was the impetus for both *Ceres Colony Cavalier* and *Project Starmaker*.

"I built a star once. Artificially. And I can confirm that this is a possible birth place of souls," Tony responded.

CHAPTER 20

The Orb

The night of my original abduction, before my time in Peru, before Ceres or any of the Starmaker Project, I was visited by a light. Out of nowhere, a blue orb flew into my room, making a static electricity crackling sound, until it then whizzed back out into the hallway and went downstairs. There was silence for a few minutes.

And this is what's true. Everything happening in the moment of my abduction was terrifying. The phone was ringing violently, there was an unnaturally bright light outside, there was a craft buzzing outside the house. I could hear my mom getting up then weirdly going back to sleep, on repeat, all while talking to something.

But when I saw the orb, I felt immediate connection and loyalty. It didn't feel out of place at all – very natural actually.

"I found you. This is it. This is where it starts," she told me.

And she told me that I would like how this ends. Not to worry. She had fixed it and she had burned a favor to do it. I wouldn't believe what she'd given up for me in that favor. I just had to get through the tough part, but that I would get through the tough part. Then we both giggled.

Then she told me that she wanted to go meet my sister. She flew out the doorway and down the stairs. That was all I saw of her. I fell back to sleep.

When I reflect back on this memory, I realize that I always expected her to come back. I thought she was going to see my sister and maybe check out our house, and then that she'd be back to visit with me. But she didn't–and shortly after she left, the greys came in my room to take me. I kept feeling like the orb should be there with me, through it all, through what came next. Which was my abduction and twenty-year service.

My sister asked the next morning if we all saw the bright lights outside? But my father immediately ended the conversation and told her–told all of us– not to speak of it.

****

Did you think it was odd that you had a friend feeling with this orb? That you were giggling at such an oddity?

Yes, absolutely. I woke up the next morning very traumatized with nothing to attribute it to. And within a few weeks, I vaguely remembered the abduction and the orb. The whole scene was weird, but actually no, it felt natural to be giggling with this orb in that moment.

Do you think souls have gender?

When they incarnate, yes. As souls, no.

At what point did you remember this blue orb?

Very early on. Like I said, within a few weeks of the abduction in 1982. It gets complicated to explain from here. I remembered a future conversation with her during my time as a child in Peru, while I was drugged on the flights. From a linear standpoint, however, I was remembering something that hadn't occurred yet. Because there is no linear time in that realm.

Printed in Great Britain
by Amazon

24551379R00093